Robert Mackenzie

The United States of America

A History

Robert Mackenzie

The United States of America
A History

ISBN/EAN: 9783743336636

Manufactured in Europe, USA, Canada, Australia, Japa

Cover: Foto ©ninafisch / pixelio.de

Manufactured and distributed by brebook publishing software (www.brebook.com)

Robert Mackenzie

The United States of America

CONTENTS.

BOOK I.

I. DISCOVERY,	9
II. COLONIZATION,	16
III. VIRGINIA,	20
IV. NEW ENGLAND,	26
V. THE NEW ENGLAND PERSECUTIONS,	36
VI. WITCHCRAFT IN NEW ENGLAND,	42
VII. THE INDIANS,	45
VIII. NEW YORK,	47
IX. PENNSYLVANIA,	50
X. GEORGIA,	53
XI. SLAVERY,	57
XII. EARLY GOVERNMENT,	63

BOOK II.

I. GEORGE WASHINGTON,	66
II. BENJAMIN FRANKLIN,	70
III. THE VALLEY OF THE OHIO,	72
IV. AMERICA ON THE EVE OF THE REVOLUTION,	80
V. BUNKER HILL,	96
VI. INDEPENDENCE,	104

VII.	AT WAR,	107
VIII.	SYMPATHY BEYOND THE SEA,	112
IX.	THE WAR CONTINUES,	114
X.	THE SURRENDER AT SARATOGA,	117
XI.	HELP FROM EUROPE,	119
XII.	MAJOR ANDRE,	123
XIII.	THE CLOSE OF THE WAR,	127
XIV.	THE THIRTEEN STATES BECOME A NATION,	132
XV.	THE WAR WITH GREAT BRITAIN,	142

BOOK III.

I.	KING COTTON,	155
II.	SLAVERY,	159
III.	MISSOURI,	165
IV.	HOPE FOR THE NEGRO,	167
V.	TEXAS,	171
VI.	THE WAR WITH MEXICO,	174
VII.	CALIFORNIA,	177
VIII.	KANSAS,	180
IX.	THE UNDERGROUND RAILWAY,	184
X.	JOHN BROWN,	187
XI.	EIGHTEEN HUNDRED AND SIXTY,	191
XII.	SECESSION,	197
XIII.	THE TWO PRESIDENTS,	201

BOOK IV.

I.	THE FIRST BLOW STRUCK,	205
II.	THE BATTLE OF BULL RUN,	212
III.	THE YOUNG NAPOLEON,	217
IV.	LIBERTY TO THE CAPTIVE,	220

V. CONFEDERATE SUCCESSES,	...	230
VI. THE WAR CONTINUES,	...	233
VII. GETTYSBURG,	...	238
VIII. THE LAST CAMPAIGN,	...	244
IX. THE MURDER OF THE PRESIDENT,	...	258
X. THE LOSSES AND THE GAINS OF THE WAR,	...	261
XI. AFTER THE WAR,	...	264
XII. HOW THE AMERICANS CARED FOR THEIR SOLDIERS,		270
XIII. ENGLAND AND AMERICA,		273
XIV. REUNITED AMERICA,	...	276

THE UNITED STATES OF AMERICA.

BOOK I.

I.

DISCOVERY.

It was late in the history of the world before Europe and America became known to each other. During the first fifteen centuries of the Christian era Europe was unaware of the vast continent which lay beyond the sea. Asia had ceased to influence her. Africa had not begun. Her history was waiting for the mighty influence which America was to exercise in her affairs through all the future ages.

Men had been slow to establish completely their dominion over the sea. They learned very early to build ships. They availed themselves very early of the surprising power which the helm exerts over the movements of a ship. But, during many ages, they found no surer guidance upon the pathless sea than that which the position of the sun and the stars afforded. When clouds intervened to deprive them of this uncertain direction, they were helpless. They were thus obliged to keep the land in view, and content themselves with creeping timidly along the coast.

But at length there was discovered a stone which the wise Creator had endowed with strange properties. It was observed that a needle brought once into contact with that stone pointed ever afterwards steadfastly to the north. Men saw that with a needle thus influenced they could guide themselves at sea as surely as on land. The Mariners' Compass untied the bond which held sailors to the coast, and gave them liberty to push out into the sea.

Just when sailors were slowly learning to put confidence in the Mariners' Compass, there arose in Europe a vehement desire for the discovery of unknown countries. A sudden interest sprang up in all that was distant and unexplored. The strange fables told by travellers were greedily received. The human mind was beginning to cast off the torpor of the Middle Ages. As intelligence increased, men became increasingly eager to ascertain the form and extent of the world in which they dwelt, and to acquaint themselves with those unknown races who were their fellow-inhabitants.

Portugal and Spain, looking out upon the boundless sea, were powerfully stirred by the new impulse. The Courts of Lisbon and Madrid swarmed with adventurers who had made discoveries, or who wished the means to make them. Conspicuous among these was an enthusiast, who during eighteen years had not ceased to importune incredulous monarchs for ships and men that he might open up the secrets of the sea. He was a tall man, of grave and gentle manners, and noble though saddened look. His eye was gray, "apt to enkindle" when he spoke of those discoveries in the making of which he felt himself to be Heaven's chosen agent. He had known hardship and sorrow in his youth, and at thirty his hair was white. He was the son of a Genoese wool-comber, and his name was Christopher Columbus. In him the universal passion for discovery rose to the dignity of an inspiration.

No sailor of our time would cross the Atlantic in such ships as were given to Columbus. In size they resembled the smaller of our river and coasting vessels. Only one of them was decked. The others were open, save at the prow and stern, where cabins were built for the crew. The sailors went unwillingly and in much fear—compelled by an order from the King. With such ships and such men Columbus left the land behind him and pushed out into these unknown waters. To him there were no dangers, no difficulties—God, who had chosen him to do this work, would sustain him for its accomplishment. He sailed on the 3rd of August 1492. On the 12th of October, in the dim light of early morning, he gazed out from the deck of his little ship upon the shores of a new world. His victory was gained. His work was done. How great it was he himself never knew. He died in the belief that he had merely discovered a shorter route to India. He never enjoyed that which would have been the best recompense for all his toil—the knowledge that he had added a vast continent to the possessions of civilized men.

The revelation by Columbus of the amazing fact that there were lands beyond the great ocean, inhabited by strange races of human beings, roused to a passionate eagerness the thirst for fresh discoveries. The splendours of the newly-found world were indeed difficult to be resisted. Wealth beyond the wildest dreams of avarice could be had, it was said, for the gathering. The sands of every river sparkled with gold. The very colour of the ground showed that gold was profusely abundant. The meanest of the Indians ornamented himself with gold and jewels. The walls of the houses glittered with pearls. There was a fountain, if one might but find it, whose waters bestowed perpetual youth upon the bather. The wildest romances were greedily received, and the Old World, with its familiar and painful realities, seemed mean and hateful beside the fabled glories of the New.

Europe then enjoyed a season of unusual calm—a short respite from the habitual toil of war—as if to afford men leisure to enter on their new possession. The last of the Moors had taken his last look at Granada, and Spain had rest from her eight centuries of war. In England, the Wars of the Roses had ceased. After thirty years of hard fighting and huge waste of life and property, the fortunate English had been able to determine which branch of a certain old family was to rule over them. Henry VII., with his clear, cold head, and his heavy hand, was guiding his people somewhat forcibly towards the victories of peace. Even France tasted the joy of repose. The Reformation was at hand. While Columbus was holding his uncertain way across the great Atlantic, a boy called Martin Luther was attending school in a small German town. The time was not far off, but as yet the mind of Europe was not engrossed by those religious strifes which were soon to convulse it.

The men whose trade was fighting turned gladly in this idle time to the world where boundless wealth was to be wrung from the grasp of unwarlike barbarians. England and France had missed the splendid prize which Columbus had won for Spain. They hastened now to secure what they could. A merchant of Bristol, John Cabot, obtained permission from the King of England to make discoveries in the northern parts of America. Cabot was to bear all expenses, and the King was to receive one-fifth of the gains of the adventure. Taking with him his son Sebastian, John Cabot sailed straight westward across the Atlantic. He reached the American continent, of which he was the undoubted discoverer. The result to him was disappointing. He landed on the coast of Labrador. Being in the same latitude as England, he reasoned that he should find the same genial climate. To his astonishment he came upon a region of intolerable cold, dreary with ice and snow. John Cabot had not heard of the

1497
A.D.

Gulf Stream and its marvellous influences. He did not know that the western shores of northern Europe are rescued from perpetual winter, and warmed up to the enjoyable temperature which they possess, by an enormous river of hot water flowing between banks of cold water eastward from the Gulf of Mexico. The Cabots made many voyages afterwards, and explored the American coast from extreme north to extreme south.

The French turned their attention to the northern parts of the New World. The rich fisheries of Newfoundland attracted them. A Frenchman sailed up the great St. Lawrence river. After some failures a French settlement was established there, and for a century and a half the French peopled Canada, until the English relieved them of the ownership.

Spanish adventurers never rested from their eager search after the treasures of the new continent. An aged warrior called Ponce de Leon fitted out an expedition at his own cost. He had heard of the marvellous fountain whose waters would restore to him the years of his wasted youth. He searched in vain. The fountain would not reveal itself to the foolish old man, and he had to bear without relief the burden of his profitless years. But he found a country hitherto unseen by Europeans, which was clothed with magnificent forests, and seemed to bloom with perpetual flowers. He called it Florida. He attempted to found a colony in the paradise he had discovered. But the natives attacked him, slew many of his men, and drove the rest to their ships, carrying with them their chief, wounded to death by the arrow of an Indian.

Ferdinand de Soto had been with Pizarro in his expedition to Peru, and returned to Spain enriched by his share of the plunder. He did not doubt that in the north were cities as rich and barbarians as confiding. An expedition to discover new regions, and plunder their inhabitants, was fitted out under his command. No one doubted that success equal to that of Cortes and Pizarro would attend this new adventure. The youth of Spain were eager to be permitted to go, and they sold houses and lands to buy them the needful equipment. Six hundred men, in the prime of life, were chosen from the crowd of applicants, and the expedition sailed, high in courage, splendid in aspect, boundless in expectation. They landed on the coast of Florida, and began their march into the wilderness. They had fetters for the Indians whom they meant to take captive. They had bloodhounds, lest these captives should escape. The camp swarmed with priests, and as they marched the festivals and processions enjoined by the Church were devoutly observed.

1539 A.D.

From the outset it was a toilsome and perilous enterprise; but to the Spaniard of that time danger was a joy. The Indians were warlike, and generally hostile. De Soto had pitched battles to fight and heavy losses to bear. Always he was victorious, but he could ill afford the cost of many such victories. The captive Indians amused him with tales of regions where gold abounded. They had learned that ignorance on that subject was very hazardous. De Soto had stimulated their knowledge by burning to death some who denied the existence of gold in that country. The Spaniards wandered slowly northwards. They looked eagerly for some great city, the plunder of whose palaces and temples would enrich them all. They found nothing better than occasionally an Indian town, composed of a few miserable huts. It was all they could do to get needful food. At length they came to a magnificent river. European eyes had seen no such river till now. It was about a mile in breadth, and its mass of water swept downward to the sea with a current of amazing strength. It was the Mississippi. The Spaniards built vessels and ferried themselves to the western bank.

There they resumed their wanderings. De Soto would not yet admit that he had failed. He still hoped that the plunder of a rich city would reward his toils. For many months the Spaniards strayed among the swamps and dense forests of that dreary region. The natives showed at first some disposition to be helpful. But the Spaniards, in their disappointment, were pitiless and savage. They amused themselves by inflicting pain upon the prisoners. They cut off their hands; they hunted them with bloodhounds; they burned them at the stake. The Indians became dangerous. De Soto hoped to awe them by claiming to be one of the gods. But the imposture was too palpable. "How can a man be God when he cannot get bread to eat?" asked a sagacious savage. It was now three years since De Soto had landed in America. The utter failure of the expedition would no longer conceal, and the men wished to return home. Broken in spirit and in frame, De Soto caught fever and died. His soldiers felled a tree and scooped room within its trunk for the body of the ill-fated adventurer. They could not bury their chief on land, lest the Indians should dishonour his remains. In the silence of midnight the rude coffin was sunk in the Mississippi, and the discoverer of the great river slept beneath its waters. The Spaniards promptly resolved now to make their way to Cuba. They had tools, and wood was abundant. They slew their horses for flesh; they plundered the Indians for bread; they struck the fetters from their prisoners to reinforce their scanty supply of iron. They built ships enough to float them down the Mississippi. Three hundred ragged and disheartened men were all that remained of the brilliant company whose hopes had been so high, whose good fortune had been so much envied.

II.

COLONIZATION.

For many years European adventurers continued to resort to the American coast in the hope of finding the way to immediate wealth. Some feeble attempts had been made to colonize. Here and there a few families had been planted. But hunger or the Indians always extinguished those infant settlements. The great idea of colonizing America was slow to take possession of European minds. The Spaniard sought for Indians to plunder. The Englishman believed in gold-mines and the north-west passage to India. It was not till America had been known for a hundred years that men began to think of finding a home beyond the Atlantic.

The courage and endurance of the early voyagers excite our wonder. Few of them sailed in ships so large as a hundred tons burthen. The merchant ships of that time were very small. The royal navies of Europe contained large vessels, but commerce was too poor to employ any but the smallest. The commerce of imperial Rome employed ships which even now would be deemed large. St. Paul was wrecked in a ship of over five hundred tons burthen. Josephus sailed in a ship of nearly one thousand tons. Europe contented herself, as yet, with vessels of a very different class. A ship of forty or fifty tons was deemed sufficient by the daring adventurers who sought to reach the Land of Promise beyond the great sea. Occasionally toy-ships of twenty or twenty-five tons were used.

The brother of Sir Walter Raleigh crossed the Atlantic in such a ship, and perished in it as he attempted to return to England.

It was not a pleasant world which the men and women of Europe had to live in during the sixteenth century. Fighting was the constant occupation of the Kings of that time. A year of peace was a rare and somewhat wearisome exception. Kings habitually, at their own unquestioned pleasure, gathered their subjects together, and marched them off to slay and plunder their neighbours. Civil wars were frequent. In these confused strifes men slew their acquaintances and friends as the only method they knew of deciding who was to fill the throne. Feeble Commerce was crushed under the iron heel of War. No such thing as security for life or property was expected. The fields of the husbandman were trodden down by the march of armies. Disbanded or deserted soldiers wandered as "masterless men" over the country, and robbed and murdered at their will. Highwaymen abounded — although highways could scarcely be said to exist. Epidemic diseases of strange type, the result of insufficient feeding and the poisonous air of undrained lands and filthy streets, desolated all European countries. Under what hardships and miseries the men of the sixteenth century passed their days, it is scarcely possible for us now to conceive.

The English Parliament once reminded James I. of certain "undoubted rights" which they possessed. The King told them, in reply, that he "did not like this style of talking, but would rather hear them say that all their privileges were derived by the grace and permission of the sovereign." Europe, during the sixteenth century, had no better understanding of the matter than James had. It was not supposed that the King was made for the people. It seemed rather to be thought that the people were made for the King. Here and there some man wiser than ordinary perceived the truth, so familiar to us, that a King is merely a great officer appointed by the people to do certain work for them. There was a Glasgow professor who taught in those dark days that the authority of the King was derived from the people, and ought to be used for their good. Two of his pupils were John Knox the reformer, and George Buchanan the historian, by whom this doctrine, so great and yet so simple, was clearly perceived and firmly maintained. But to the great mass of mankind it seemed that the King had divine authority to dispose of his subjects and their property according to his pleasure. Poor patient humanity still bowed in lowly reverence before its Kings, and bore, without wondering or murmuring, all that it pleased them to inflict. No stranger superstition has ever possessed the human mind than this boundless mediæval veneration for the King—a veneration which follies the most abject, vices the most enormous, were not able to quench.

But as this unhappy century draws towards its close, the elements of a most benign change are plainly seen at work. The Bible has been largely read. The Bible is the book of all ages and of all circumstances. But never, surely, since its first gift to man was it more needful to any age than to that which now welcomed its restoration with wonder and delight. It took deep hold on the minds of men. It exercised a silent influence which gradually changed the aspect of society. The narrative portions of Scripture were especially acceptable to the untutored intellect of that time; and thus the Old Testament was preferred to the New. This preference led to some mistakes. Rules which had been given to an ancient Asiatic people were applied in circumstances for which they were never intended or fitted. It is easy to smile at these mistakes. But it is impossible to over-estimate the social and political good which we now enjoy as a result of this incessant reading of the Bible by the people of the sixteenth century.

In nearly all European countries the King claimed to regulate the religious belief of his subjects. Even in England that power was still claimed. The people were beginning to suspect that they were entitled to think for themselves—a suspicion which grew into an indignant certainty, and widened and deepened till it swept from the throne the unhappy House of Stuart.

A little way into the seventeenth century America became the refuge of those who would not receive their faith at the bidding of the King. The best part of American colonization resulted from the foolish and insolent oppressions of Europe. At the beginning, however, it was not so. It was from an impulse of vagrant blackguardism that the first American colony sprang.

III.

VIRGINIA.

Sir Walter Raleigh spent a large fortune in attempting to colonize Virginia. He succeeded in directing the attention of his countrymen to the region which had kindled his own enthusiasm. But his colonies never prospered. Sometimes the colonists returned home disgusted by the hardships of the wilderness. Once they were massacred by the Indians. When help came from England the infant settlement was in ruins. The bones of unburied men lay about the fields; wild deer strayed among the untenanted houses. Once a colony wholly disappeared. To this day its fate is unknown.

Sir Walter was enduring his long captivity in the Tower, writing his "History of the World," and moaning piteously over the havoc which prison-damps wrought upon his handsome frame. The time had now come, and his labours were about to bear fruit. The history of Virginia was about to open. It opened with meagre promise. A charter from the King established a Company whose function was to colonize—whose privilege was to trade. The Company sent out an expedition which sailed in three small vessels. It consisted of one hundred and five men. Of these one-half were gentlemen of broken fortune. Some were tradesmen; others were footmen. Only a very few were farmers, or mechanics, or persons in any way fitted for the life they sought. Morally the aspect of the expedition was even more discouraging. "An

1606
A.D.

hundred dissolute persons" were on board the ships. The respectable portions of the expedition must have gone into very little room.

But, happily for Virginia, there sailed with these reprobate founders of a new empire a man whom Providence had highly gifted with fitness to govern his fellow-men. His name was John Smith. No writer of romance would have given his hero this name. But, in spite of his name, the man was truly heroic. He was still under thirty, a strong-limbed, deep-chested, massively-built man. From boyhood he had been a soldier—roaming over the world in search of adventures, wherever hard blows were being exchanged. He was mighty in single combat. Once, while opposing armies looked on, he vanquished three Turks, and, like David, cut off their heads, and bore them to his tent. Returning to England when the passion for colonizing was at its height, he caught at once the prevailing impulse. He joined the Virginian expedition. Ultimately he became its chief. His fitness was so manifest, that no reluctance on his own part, no jealousies on that of his companions, could bar him from the highest place. Men became Kings of old by the same process which now made Smith a chief.

The "dissolute persons" sailed in their ships up the James river. Landing there, they proceeded to construct a little town, which they named Jamestown, in honour of the King. This was the first colony which struck its roots in American soil. The colonists were charmed with the climate and with the luxuriant beauty of the wilderness on whose confines they had settled. But as yet it was only a wilderness. The forest had to be cleared that food might be grown. The exiled gentlemen laboured manfully, but under grievous discouragements. "The axes so oft blistered their tender fingers, that many times every third blow had a loud oath to drown the echo." Smith was a man upon whose soul there lay a becoming reverence for sacred things. He devised how to have every man's oaths numbered; "and at night, for every oath, to have a can of water poured down his sleeve." Under this treatment the evil assuaged.

The emigrants had landed in early spring. Summer came with its burning heat. Supplies of food ran low. "Had we been as free from all sins as from gluttony and drunkenness," Smith wrote, "we might have been canonized as saints." The colonists sickened and died. From those poor blistered fingers dropped for ever the unaccustomed axe. Before autumn every second man had died. But the hot Virginian sun, which proved so deadly to the settlers, ripened the wheat they had sowed in the spring, and freed the survivors from the pressure of want. Winter brought them a healthier temperature and abundant supplies of wild-fowl and game.

When the welfare of the colony was in some measure secured, Smith set forth with a few companions to explore the interior of the country. He and his followers were captured by the Indians. The followers were summarily butchered. Smith's composure did not fail him in the worst extremity. He produced his pocket-compass, and interested the savages by explaining its properties. He wrote a letter in their sight—to their infinite wonder. They spared him, and made a show of him in all the settlements round about. He was to them an unfathomable mystery. He was plainly superhuman. Whether his power would bring to them good or evil, they were not able to determine. After much hesitation they chose the course which prudence seem to counsel. They resolved to extinguish powers so formidable, regarding whose use they could obtain no guarantee. Smith was bound and stretched upon the earth, his head resting upon a great stone. The mighty club was uplifted to dash out his brains. But Smith was a man who won golden opinions of all. The Indian chief had a daughter, Pocahontas, a child of ten or twelve years. She could not bear to see the pleasing Englishman destroyed. As Smith lay waiting the fatal stroke, she caught him in her arms and interposed herself between him and the club. Her intercession prevailed, and Smith was set free.

Five years later, "an honest and discreet" young Englishman called John Rolfe loved this young Indian girl. He had a sore mental struggle about uniting himself with "one of barbarous breeding and of a cursed race." But love triumphed. He laboured for her conversion, and had the happiness of seeing her baptized in the little church of Jamestown. Then he married her. After a time he took her home to England. Her appearance was pleasing; her mind was acute; her piety was sincere; her manners bore picturesque evidence of her forest upbringing. The English King and Court regarded her with lively interest as the first-fruits of the wilderness. Great hopes were founded on this union of the two races. She is the brightest picture—this young Virginian wife and mother—which the history of the doomed native races presents to us. But she did not live to revisit her native land. Death parted her very early from her husband and her child.

When Smith returned from captivity the colony was on the verge of extinction. Only thirty-eight persons were left, and they were preparing to depart. With Smith, hope returned to the despairing settlers. They resumed their work, confident in the resources of their chief. Fresh arrivals from England cheered them. The character of these reinforcements had not as yet improved. "Vagabond gentlemen" formed still a large majority of the settlers—many of them, we are told, "packed off to escape worse destinies at home." The colony, thus composed, had already gained a very bad reputation: so bad that some, rather than be sent there, "chose to be hanged, *and were.*" Over these most undesirable subjects Smith ruled with an authority which no man dared or desired to question. But he was severely injured by an accidental explosion of gunpowder. Surgical aid was not in the colony. Smith required to go to England, and once more hungry ruin settled down upon Virginia.

1610
A.D.

In six months the five hundred men whom Smith had left dwindled to sixty. These were already embarked and departing, when they were met by Lord Delaware, the new governor. Once more the colony was saved.

Years of quiet growth succeeded. Emigrants—not wholly now of the dissolute sort—flowed steadily in. Bad people bore rule in England during most of the seventeenth century, and they sold the good people to be slaves in Virginia. The victims of the brutal Judge Jeffreys—the Scotch Covenanters taken at Bothwell Bridge—were shipped off to this profitable market. In 1688 the population of Virginia had increased to 50,000. The little wooden capital swelled out. Other little wooden towns established themselves. Deep in the unfathomed wilderness rose the huts of adventurous settlers, in secluded nooks, by the banks of nameless Virginian streams. A semblance of roads connected the youthful communities. The Indians were relentlessly suppressed. The Virginians bought no land. They took what they required—slaying or expelling the former occupants. Perhaps there were faults on both sides. Once the Indians planned a massacre so cunningly that over three hundred Englishmen perished before the bloody hand of the savages could be stayed.

The early explorers of Virginia found tobacco in extensive use among the Indians. It was the chief medicine of the savages. Its virtues—otherwise unaccountable—were supposed to proceed from a spiritual presence whose home was in the plant. Tobacco was quickly introduced into England. It rose rapidly into favour. Men who had heretofore smoked only hemp knew how to prize tobacco. King James wrote vehemently against it. He issued a proclamation against trading in an article which was corrupting to mind and body. He taxed it heavily when he could not exclude it. The Pope excommunicated all who smoked in churches. But, in defiance of law and reason, the demand for tobacco continued to increase.

The Virginians found their most profitable occupation in supplying this demand. So eager were they, that tobacco was grown in the squares and streets of Jamestown. In the absence of money tobacco became the Virginian currency. Accounts were kept in tobacco. The salaries of members of Assembly, the stipends of clergymen, were paid in tobacco. Offences were punished by fines expressed in tobacco. Absence from church cost the delinquent fifty pounds; refusing to have his child baptized, two thousand pounds; entertaining a Quaker, five thousand pounds. When the stock of tobacco was unduly large, the currency was debased, and much inconvenience resulted. The Virginians corrected this evil in their monetary system by compelling every planter to burn a certain proportion of his stock.

Within a few years of the settlement the Virginians had a written Constitution, according to which they were ruled. They had a Parliament chosen by the burghs, and a Governor sent them from England. The Episcopal Church was established among them, and the colony divided into parishes. A College was erected for the use not only of the English, but also of the most promising young Indians. But they never became an educated people. The population was widely scattered, so that schools were almost impossible. In respect of education, Virginia fell far behind her sisters in the North.

IV.

NEW ENGLAND.

A LITTLE more than two centuries ago New England was one vast forest. Here and there a little space was cleared, a little corn was raised; a few Indian families made their temporary abode. The savage occupants of the land spent their profitless lives to no better purpose than in hunting and fighting. The rivers which now give life to so much cheerful industry flowed uselessly to the sea. Providence had prepared a home which a great people might fitly inhabit. Let us see whence and how the men were brought who were the destined possessors of its opulence.

The Reformation had taught that every man is entitled to read his Bible for himself, and guide his life by the light he obtains from it. But the lesson was too high to be soon learned. Protestant princes no more than Popish could permit their subjects to think for themselves. James I. had just ascended the English throne. His was the head of a fool and the heart of a tyrant. He would allow no man to separate himself from the Established Church. He would "harry out of the land" all who attempted such a thing. And he was as good as his word. Men would separate from the Church, and the King stretched out his pitiless hand to crush them.

On the northern borders of Nottinghamshire stands the little town of Scrooby. Here there were some grave and well-reputed persons, to whom the idle ceremonies of the Established Church were an offence. They met in secret at the house of one of their number, a gentleman named Brewster. They were ministered to in all scriptural simplicity by the pastor of their choice —Mr. Robinson, a wise and good man. But their secret meetings were betrayed to the authorities, and their lives were made bitter by the persecutions that fell upon them. They resolved to leave their own land and seek among strangers that freedom which was denied them at home.

They embarked with all their goods for Holland. But when the ship was about to sail, soldiers came upon them, plundered them, and drove them on shore. They were marched to the public square of Boston, and there the Fathers of New England endured such indignities as an unbelieving rabble could inflict. After some weeks in prison they were suffered to return home.

Next spring they tried again to escape. This time a good many were on board, and the others were waiting for the return of the boat which would carry them to the ship. Suddenly dragoons were seen spurring across the sands. The shipmaster pulled up his anchor and pushed out to sea with those of his passengers whom he had. The rest were conducted to prison. After a time they were set at liberty. In little groups they made their way to Holland. Mr. Robinson and his congregation were reunited, and the first stage of the weary pilgrimage from the Old England to the New was at length accomplished.

Eleven quiet and not unprosperous years were spent in Holland. The Pilgrims worked with patient industry at their various handicrafts. They quickly gained the reputation of doing honestly and effectively whatever they professed to do, and thus they found abundant employment. Mr. Brewster established a printing-press, and printed books about liberty, which, as he had the satisfaction of knowing, greatly enraged the foolish King James. The little colony

1609
A.D.

received additions from time to time as oppression in England became more intolerable.

The instinct of separation was strong within the Pilgrim heart. They could not bear the thought that their little colony was to mingle with the Dutchmen and lose its independent existence. But already their sons and daughters were forming alliances which threatened this result. The Fathers considered long and anxiously how the danger was to be averted. They determined again to go on pilgrimage. They would seek a home beyond the Atlantic, where they could dwell apart and found a State in which they should be free to think.

On a sunny morning in July the Pilgrims kneel upon the seashore at Delfthaven, while the pastor prays for the success of their journey. Out upon the gleaming sea a little ship lies waiting. Money has not been found to transplant the whole colony, and only a hundred have been sent. The remainder will follow when they can. These hundred depart amid tears and prayers and fond farewells. Mr. Robinson dismissed them with counsels which breathed a pure and high-toned wisdom. He urged them to keep their minds ever open for the reception of new truths. "The Lord," he said, "has more truth to break forth out of his holy Word. I cannot sufficiently bewail the condition of the Reformed Churches, who are come to a period in religion, and will go at present no further than the instruments of their reformation. Luther and Calvin were great and shining lights in their times, yet they penetrated not into the whole counsel of God, but, were they now living, would be as willing to embrace further light as that which they first received. I beseech you, remember that you be ready to receive whatever truth shall be made known to you from the written Word of God."

1620 A.D.

Sixty-eight years later, another famous departure from the coast of Holland took place. It was that of William, Prince of

Orange, coming to deliver England from tyranny, and give a new course to English history. A powerful fleet and army sailed with the Prince. The chief men of the country accompanied him to his ships. Public prayers for his safety were offered up in all the churches. Insignificant beside this seems at first sight the unregarded departure of a hundred working-men and women. It was in truth, however, not less, but even more memorable. For these poor people went forth to found a great empire, destined to leave as deep and as enduring a mark upon the world's history as Rome or even as England has done.

The *Mayflower*, in which the Pilgrims made their voyage, was a ship of one hundred and sixty tons. The weather proved stormy and cold; the voyage unexpectedly long. It was early in September when they sailed. It was not till the 11th November that the *Mayflower* dropped her anchor in the waters of Cape Cod Bay.

It was a bleak-looking and discouraging coast which lay before them. Nothing met the eye but low sand hills, covered with ill-grown wood down to the margin of the sea. The Pilgrims had now to choose a place for their settlement. About this they hesitated so long that the captain threatened to put them all on shore and leave them. Little expeditions were sent to explore. At first no suitable locality could be found. The men had great hardships to endure. The cold was so excessive that the spray froze upon their clothes, and they resembled men cased in armour. At length a spot was fixed upon. The soil appeared to be good, and abounded in "delicate springs" of water. On the 23rd December the Pilgrims landed—stepping ashore upon a huge boulder of granite, which is still reverently preserved by their descendants. Here they resolved to found their settlement, which they agreed to call New Plymouth.

The winter was severe, and the infant colony was brought very near to extinction. They had been badly fed on board the

Mayflower, and for some time after going on shore there was very imperfect shelter from the weather. Sickness fell heavily on the worn-out Pilgrims. Every second day a grave had to be dug in the frozen ground. By the time spring came in there were only fifty survivors, and these sadly enfeebled and dispirited.

But all through this dismal winter the Pilgrims laboured at their heavy task. The care of the sick, the burying of the dead, sadly hindered their work. But the building of their little town went on. They found that nineteen houses would contain their diminished numbers. These they built. Then they surrounded them with a palisade. Upon an eminence beside their town they erected a structure which served a double purpose. Above, it was a fort, on which they mounted six cannon; below, it was their church. Hitherto the Indians had been a cause of anxiety, but had done them no harm. Now they felt safe. Indeed there had never been much risk. A recent epidemic had swept off nine-tenths of the Indians who inhabited that region, and the discouraged survivors could ill afford to incur the hostility of their formidable visitors.

The Pilgrims had been careful to provide for themselves a government. They had drawn up and signed, in the cabin of the *Mayflower*, a document forming themselves into a body politic, and promising obedience to all laws framed for the general good. Under this Constitution they appointed John Carver to be their Governor. They dutifully acknowledged King James, but they left no very large place for his authority. They were essentially a self-governing people. They knew what despotism was, and they were very sure that democracy could by no possibility be so bad.

The welcome spring came at length, and " the birds sang in the woods most pleasantly." The health of the colony began somewhat to improve, but there was still much suffering to endure. The summer passed not unprosperously. They had taken possession of the deserted clearings of the Indians, and had no difficulty in providing themselves with food. But in the autumn came a ship with a new company of Pilgrims. This was very encouraging, but unhappily the ship brought no provisions, and the supplies of the colonists were not sufficient for this unexpected addition. For six months there was only half allowance to each. Such straits recurred frequently during the first two or three years. Often the colonists knew not at night "where to have a bit in the morning." Once or twice the opportune arrival of a ship saved them from famishing. They suffered much, but their cheerful trust in Providence and in their own final triumph never wavered. They faced the difficulties of their position with undaunted hearts. Slowly but surely the little colony struck its roots and began to grow.

The years which followed the coming of the Pilgrims were years through which good men in England found it bitter to live. Charles the First was upon the throne. Laud was Archbishop of Canterbury. Bigotry as blind and almost as cruel as England had ever seen thus sat in her high places. Dissent from the Popish usages, which prevailed more and more in the Church, was at the peril of life. A change was near. John Hampden was farming his lands in Buckinghamshire. A greater than he—his cousin, Oliver Cromwell—was leading his quiet rural life at Huntingdon, not without many anxious and indignant thoughts about the evils of his time. John Milton was peacefully writing his minor poems, and filling his mind with the learning of the ancients. The Men had come, and the Hour was at hand. But as yet King Charles and Archbishop Laud had it all their own way. They fined and imprisoned every man who ventured to think otherwise than they wished him to think: they slit his nose, they cut off his ears, they gave him weary hours in the pillory. They ordered that men should not leave the kingdom without the King's permission. Eight ships lay in the Thames, with their passengers on board, when that order was given forth. The soldiers cleared the ships, and the poor emigrants were driven back, in poverty and despair, to endure the misery from which they were so eager to escape.

New England was the refuge to which the wearied victims of this senseless tyranny looked. The Pilgrims wrote to their friends at home, and every letter was regarded with the interest due to a "sacred script." They had hardships to tell of at first; then they had prosperity and comfort; always they had liberty. New England seemed a paradise to men who were denied permission to worship God according to the manner which they deemed right. Every summer a few ships were freighted for the settlements. Many of the silenced ministers came. Many of their congregations came, glad to be free, at whatever sacrifice, from the tyranny which disgraced their native land. The region around New Plymouth became too narrow for the population. From time to time a little party would go forth, with a minister at its head. With wives and children and baggage they crept slowly through the swampy forest. By a week or two of tedious journeying they reached some point which pleased their fancy, or to which they judged that Providence had sent them. There they built their little town, with its wooden huts, its palisade, its fort—on which one or two guns were ultimately mounted. Thus were founded many of the cities of New England.

For some years the difficulties which the colonists encountered were almost overwhelming. There seemed at times even to be danger that death by starvation would end the whole enterprise. But they were a stout-hearted, patient, industrious people, and labour gradually brought comfort. The virgin soil began to yield them abundant harvests. They fished with such success that they manured their fields with the harvest of the sea. They spun and they weaved. They felled the timber of their boundless forests. They built ships, and sent away to foreign countries the timber, the fish, the furs which were not required at home. Ere many years a ship built in Massachusetts sailed for London, followed by "many prayers of the churches." Their infant commerce was not without its troubles. They had little or no coin. Indian corn was made a legal tender. Bullets were legalized in room of the farthings which, with their other coins, had vanished to pay for foreign goods. But no difficulty could long resist their steady, undismayed labour.

1643 A.D.

They were a noble people who had thus begun to strike their roots in the great forests of New England. Their peculiarities may indeed amuse us. The Old Testament was their statute-book, and they deemed that the institutions of Moses were the best model for those of New England. They made attendance on public worship compulsory. They christened their children by Old Testament names. They regulated female attire by law. They considered long hair unscriptural, and preached against veils and wigs.

The least wise among us can smile at the mistakes into which the Puritan Fathers of New England fell. But the most wise of all ages will most profoundly reverence the purity, the earnestness, the marvellous enlightenment of these men. From their incessant study of the Bible they drew a love of human liberty unsurpassed in depth and fervour. Coming from under despotic rule, they established at once a government absolutely free. They felt—what Europe has not even yet fully apprehended—that the citizens of a State should be able to guide the affairs of that State without helpless dependence upon a few great families; that the members of a Church ought to guide the affairs of that Church, waiting for the sanction of no patron, however noble and good. It was one of their fundamental laws that all strangers professing the Christian religion and driven from their homes by persecutors, should be succoured at the public charge. The education of children was almost their earliest care. The Pilgrims bore with them across the sea a deep persuasion that their infant State could not thrive without education. Three years after the landing, it was reported of them among the friends they had left in London, that "their children were not catechised, nor taught to read." The colonists felt keenly this reproach. They utterly denied its justice. They owned, indeed, that they had not yet attained to a school, much as they desired it. But all parents did their best, each in the education of his own children. In a very few years schools began to appear. Such endowment as could be afforded was freely given. Some tolerably qualified brother was fixed upon, and "entreated to become schoolmaster." And thus gradually the foundations were laid of the noble school system of New England. Soon a law was passed that every town containing fifty householders must have a common school; every town of a hundred householders must have a grammar school. Harvard College was established within fifteen years of the landing.

The founders of New England were men who had known at home the value of letters. Brewster carried with him a library of two hundred and seventy-five volumes, and his was not the largest collection in the colony. The love of knowledge was deep and universal. New England has never swerved from her early loyalty to the cause of education.

Every colonist was necessarily a soldier. The State provided him with arms, if poor; required him to provide himself, if rich. His weapons were sword, pike, and matchlock, with a forked stick on which to rest his artillery in taking aim. The people were carefully trained to the use of arms. In the devout spirit of the time, their drills were frequently opened and closed with prayer.

Twenty-three years after the landing of the Pilgrims the population of New England had grown to 24,000. Forty-nine little wooden towns, with their wooden churches, wooden forts, and wooden ramparts, were dotted here and there over the land. There were four separate colonies, which hitherto had maintained separate governments. They were Plymouth, Massachusetts, Connecticut, and New Haven. There appeared at first a disposition in the Pilgrim mind to scatter widely, and remain apart in small self-governing communities. For some years every little band which pushed deeper into the wilderness settled itself into an independent State, having no political relations with its neighbours. But this isolation could not continue. The wilderness had other inhabitants, whose presence was a standing menace. Within "striking distance" there were Indians enough to trample out the solitary little English communities. On their frontiers were Frenchmen and Dutchmen—natural enemies, as all men in that time were to each other. For mutual defence and encouragement, the four colonies joined themselves into the United Colonies of New England. This was the first confederation in a land where confederations of unprecedented magnitude were hereafter to be established.

1643
A.D.

V.

THE NEW ENGLAND PERSECUTIONS.

The Puritans left their native England and came to the "outside of the world," as they called it, that they might enjoy liberty to worship God according to the way which they deemed right. They had discovered that they themselves were entitled to toleration. They felt that the restraints laid upon themselves were very unjust and very grievous. But their light as yet led them no further. They had not discovered that people who differed from them were as well entitled to be tolerated as they themselves were. We have no right to blame them for their backwardness. Simple as it seems, men have not all found out, even yet, that every one of them is fully entitled to think for himself.

And thus it happened that, before the Pilgrims had enjoyed for many years the cheerful liberty of their new home, **1631** doctrines raised their heads among them which they A.D. felt themselves bound to suppress. One February day there stepped ashore at Boston a young man upon whose coming great issues depended. His name was Roger Williams. He was a clergyman—"godly and zealous"—a man of rare virtue and power. Cromwell admitted him, in later years, to a considerable measure of intimacy. He was the friend of John Milton—in the bright days of the poet's youth, ere yet "the ever-during dark" surrounded him. From him Milton acquired his knowledge of the Dutch language. He carried with him to the New World certain strange opinions. Long thought had satisfied him that in regard to religious belief and worship man is responsible to God alone. No man, said Williams, is entitled to lay compulsion upon another man in regard to religion. The civil power has to do only with the "bodies and goods and outward estates" of men. In the domain of conscience God is the only ruler. New England was not able to receive these sentiments. Williams became minister at Salem, where he was held in high account. In time his opinions drew down upon him the unfavourable notice of the authorities. The General Court of Massachusetts brought him to trial for the errors of his belief. His townsmen and congregation deserted him. His wife reproached him bitterly with the evil he was bringing upon his family. Mr. Williams could do no otherwise. He must testify with his latest breath, if need be, against the "soul oppression" which he saw around him. The court heard him, discovered error in his opinions, declared him guilty, and pronounced upon him sentence of banishment.

All honour to this good and brave, if somewhat eccentric man. He of all the men of his time saw most clearly the beauty of absolute freedom in matters of conscience. He went forth from Salem. He obtained a grant of land from the Indians, and he founded the State of Rhode Island. Landing one day from a boat in which he explored his new possessions, he climbed a gentle slope, and rested with his companions beside a spring. It seemed to him that the capital of his infant State ought to be here. He laid the foundations of his city, which he named Providence, in grateful recognition of the power which had guided his uncertain steps. His settlement was to be "a shelter for persons distressed for conscience." Most notably has it been so. Alone of all the States of Christendom, Rhode Island has no taint of persecution in her statute-book or in her history. Massachusetts continued to drive out her heretics. Rhode

Island took them in. They might err in their interpretation of Scripture. Pity for themselves if they did so. But while they obeyed the laws, they might interpret Scripture according to the light they had. Many years after, Mr. Williams became President of the colony which he had founded. The neighbouring States were at that time sharply chastising the Quakers with lash and branding-iron and gibbet. Rhode Island was invited to join in the persecution. Mr. Williams replied that he had no law whereby to punish any for their belief "as to salvation and an eternal condition." He abhorred the doctrines of the Quakers. In his seventy-third year he rowed thirty miles in an open boat to wage a public debate with some of the advocates of the system. Thus and thus only could he resist the progress of opinions which he deemed pernicious. In beautiful consistency and completeness stands out to the latest hour of his long life this good man's loyalty to the absolute liberty of the human conscience.

And thus, too, it happened that when seven or eight men began to deny that infants should be baptized, New England never doubted that she did right in forcibly trampling out their heresy. The heretics had started a meeting of their own, where they might worship God apart from those who baptized their infants. One Sabbath morning the constable invaded their worship and forcibly bore them away to church. Their deportment there was not unsuitable to the manner of their inbringing. They audaciously clapped on their hats while the minister prayed, and made no secret that they deemed it sin to join in the services of those who practised infant baptism. For this "separation of themselves from God's people" they were put on trial. They were fined, and some of the more obdurate among them were ordered to be "well whipped." We have no reason to doubt that this order was executed in spirit as well as in letter. And then a

1651
A.D.

law went forth that every man who openly condemned the baptizing of infants should suffer banishment. Thus resolute were the good men of New England that the right which they had come so far to enjoy should not be enjoyed by any one who saw a different meaning from theirs in any portion of the Divine Word.

Thus, too, when Massachusetts had reason to apprehend the coming of certain followers of the Quaker persuasion, she was smitten with a great fear. A fast-day was proclaimed, that the alarmed people might "seek the face of God in reference to the abounding of errors, especially those of the Ranters and Quakers." As they fasted, a ship was nearing their shores with certain Quaker women on board. These unwelcome visitors were promptly seized and lodged in prison; their books were burned by the hangman; they themselves were sent away home by the ships which brought them. All ship-masters were strictly forbidden to bring Quakers to the colony. A poor woman, the wife of a London tailor, left her husband and her children, to bring, as she said, a message from the Lord to New England. Her trouble was but poorly bestowed; for they to whom her message came requited her with twenty stripes and instant banishment. The banished Quakers took the earliest opportunity of finding their way back. Laws were passed dooming to death all who ventured to return. A poor fanatic was following his plough in distant Yorkshire, when the word of the Lord came to him saying, "Go to Boston." He went, and the ungrateful men of Boston hanged him. Four persons in all suffered death. Many were whipped. Some had their ears cut off. But public opinion, which has always been singularly humane in America, began to condemn these foolish cruelties. And the Quakers had friends at home—friends who had access at Court. There came a letter in the King's name directing that

1656 A.D.

1661 A.D.

the authorities of New England should "forbear to proceed further against the Quakers." That letter came by the hands of a Quaker who was under sentence of death if he dared to return. The authorities could not but receive it—could not but give effect to it. The persecution ceased; and with it may be said to close, in America, all forcible interference with the right of men to think for themselves.

The Quakers, as they are known to us, are of all sects the least offensive. A persecution of this serene, thoughtful, self-restrained people, may well surprise us. But, in justice to New England, it must be told that the first generation of Quakers differed extremely from succeeding generations. They were a fanatical people — extravagant, disorderly, rejecters of lawful authority. A people more intractable, more unendurable by any government, never lived. They were guided by an "inner light," which habitually placed them at variance with the laws of the country in which they lived, as well as with the most harmless social usages. George Fox declared that "the Lord forbade him to put off his hat to any man." His followers were inconveniently and provokingly aggressive. They invaded public worship. They openly expressed their contempt for the religion of their neighbours. They perpetually came with "messages from the Lord," which it was not pleasant to listen to. They appeared in public places very imperfectly attired, thus symbolically to express and to rebuke the spiritual nakedness of the time. After a little, when their zeal allied itself with discretion, they became a most valuable element in American society. But we can scarcely wonder that they created alarm at first. The men of New England took a very simple view of the subject. They had bought and paid for every acre of soil which they occupied. Their country was a homestead from which they might exclude whom they chose. They would not receive men whose object was to overthrow all their institutions, civil and religious. It was a mistake, but a most natural mistake. Long afterwards, when New England saw her error, she nobly made what amends she could, by giving compensation to the representatives of those Quakers who had suffered in the evil times.

VI.

WITCHCRAFT IN NEW ENGLAND.

When the Pilgrims left their native land, the belief in witchcraft was universal. England, in much fear, busied herself with the slaughter of friendless old women who were suspected of an alliance with Satan. King James had published his book on Demonology a few years before, in which he maintained that to forbear from putting witches to death was an "odious treason against God." England was no wiser than her King. All during James's life, and long after he had ceased from invading the kingdom of Satan, the yearly average of executions for witchcraft was somewhere about five hundred.

The Pilgrims carried with them across the Atlantic the universal delusion. Their way of life was fitted to strengthen it. They lived on the verge of vast and gloomy forests. The howl of the wolf and the scream of the panther sounded nightly around their cabins. Treacherous savages lurked in the woods watching the time to plunder and to slay. Every circumstance was fitted to increase the susceptibility of the mind to gloomy and superstitious impressions. But for the first quarter of a century, while every ship brought news of witch-killing at home, no Satanic outbreak disturbed the settlers. The sense of brotherhood was yet too strong among them. Men who have braved great dangers and endured great hardships together, do not readily come to look upon each other as the allies and agents of the Evil One.

In 1645 four persons were put to death for witchcraft. During the next half century there occur at intervals solitary cases, when some unhappy wretch falls a victim to the lurking superstition. It was in 1692 that witch-slaying burst forth in its epidemic form, and with a fury which has seldom been witnessed elsewhere.

In the State of Massachusetts there is a little town, then called Salem, sitting pleasantly in a plain between two rivers; and in the town of Salem there dwelt at that time a minister whose name was Paris. In the month of February the daughter and niece of Mr. Paris became ill. It was a dark time for Massachusetts; for the colony was at war with the French and Indians, and was suffering cruelly from their ravages. The doctors sat in solemn conclave on the afflicted girls, and pronounced them bewitched. Mr. Paris, not doubting that it was even so, bestirred himself to find the offenders. Suspicion fell upon three old women, who were at once seized. And then, with marvellous rapidity, the mania spread. The rage and fear of the distracted community swelled high. Every one suspected his neighbour. Children accused their parents. Parents accused their children. The prisons could scarcely contain the suspected. The town of Falmouth hanged its minister, a man of intelligence and worth. Some near relations of the Governor were denounced. Even the beasts were not safe. A dog was solemnly put to death for the part he had taken in some Satanic festivity.

For more than twelve months this mad panic raged in the New England States. It is just to say that the hideous cruelties which were practised in Europe were not resorted to in the prosecution of American witches. Torture was not inflicted to wring confession from the victim. The American test was more humane, and not more foolish, than the European. Those suspected persons who denied their guilt, were judged guilty and hanged. Those who confessed were, for the most part, set free. Many hundreds of innocent persons, who scorned to purchase life by falsehood, perished miserably under the fury of an excited people.

The fire had been kindled in a moment; it was extinguished as suddenly. The Governor of Massachusetts only gave effect to the reaction which had occurred in the public mind, when he abruptly stopped all prosecutions against witches, dismissed all the suspected, pardoned all the condemned. The House of Assembly proclaimed a fast—entreating that God would pardon the errors of His people " in a late tragedy raised by Satan and his instruments." One of the judges stood up in church in Boston, with bowed down head and sorrowful countenance, while a paper was read, in which he begged the prayers of the congregation, that the innocent blood which he had erringly shed might not be visited on the country or on him. The Salem jury asked forgiveness of God and the community for what they had done under the power of " a strong and general delusion." Poor Mr. Paris was now at a sad discount. He made public acknowledgment of his error. But at his door lay the origin of all this slaughter of the unoffending. His part in the tragedy could not be forgiven. The people would no longer endure his ministry, and demanded his removal. Mr. Paris resigned his charge, and went forth from Salem a broken man.

If the error of New England was great and most lamentable, her repentance was prompt and deep. Five-and-twenty years after she had clothed herself in sackcloth, old women were still burned to death for witchcraft in Great Britain. The year of blood was never repeated in America

VII.

THE INDIANS.

The great continent on which the Pilgrims had landed was the home of innumerable tribes of Indians. They had no settled abode. The entire nation wandered hither and thither as their fancy or their chances of successful hunting directed. When the wood was burned down in their neighbourhood, or the game became scarce, they abandoned their villages and moved off to a more inviting region. They had their great warriors, their great battles, their brilliant victories, their crushing defeats— all as uninteresting to mankind as the wars of the kites and crows. They were a race of tall, powerful men—copper-coloured, with hazel eye, high cheek-bone, and coarse black hair. In manner they were grave, and not without a measure of dignity. They had courage, but it was of that kind which is greater in suffering than in doing. They were a cunning, treacherous, cruel race, among whom the slaughter of women and children took rank as a great feat of arms. They had almost no laws, and for religious beliefs a few of the most grovelling superstitions. They worshipped the Devil because he was wicked, and might do them an injury. Civilization could lay no hold upon them. They quickly learned to use the white man's musket. They never learned to use the tools of the white man's industry. They developed a love for intoxicating drink passionate and irresistible beyond all example. The settlers behaved to them as Christian men should. They took no land from them. What land they required they bought and paid for. Every acre of

New England soil was come by with scrupulous honesty. The friendship of the Indians was anxiously cultivated—sometimes from fear, oftener from pity. But nothing could stay their progress towards extinction. Inordinate drunkenness and the gradual limitation of their hunting-grounds told fatally on their numbers. And occasionally the English were forced to march against some tribe which refused to be at peace, and to inflict a defeat which left few survivors.

Early in the history of New England, efforts were made to win the Indians to the Christian faith. The Governor of Massachusetts appointed ministers to carry the gospel to the savages. Mr. John Eliot, the Apostle of the Indians, was a minister near Boston. Moved by the pitiful condition of the natives, he acquired the language of some of the tribes in his neighbourhood. He went and preached to them in their own tongue. He printed books for them. The savages received his words. Many of them listened to his sermons in tears. Many professed faith in Christ, and were gathered into congregations. He gave them a simple code of laws. It was even attempted to establish a college for training native teachers. But this had to be abandoned. The slothfulness of the Indian youth, and their devouring passion for strong liquors, unfitted them for the ministry. These vices seemed incurable in the Indian character. No persuasion could induce them to labour. They could be taught to rest on the Sabbath; they could not be taught to work on the other six days. And even the best of them would sell all they had for spirits. These were grave hindrances; but, in spite of them, Christianity made considerable progress among the Indians. The hold which it then gained was never altogether lost. And it was observed that in all the misunderstandings which arose between the English and the natives, the converts steadfastly adhered to their new friends.

1646 A.D.

VIII.

NEW YORK.

During the first forty years of its existence, the great city which we call New York was a Dutch settlement, known among men as New Amsterdam. That region had been discovered for the Dutch East India Company by Henry Hudson, who was still in search, as Columbus had been, of a shorter route to the East. The Dutch have never displayed any aptitude for colonizing. But they were unsurpassed in mercantile discernment, and they set up trading stations with much judgment. Three or four years after the Pilgrims landed at Plymouth, the Dutch West India Company determined to enter into trading relations with the Indians along the line of the Hudson river. They sent out a few families, who planted themselves at the southern extremity of Manhattan Island. A wooden fort was built, around which clustered a few wooden houses—just as in Europe the baron's castle arose and the huts of the baron's dependants sheltered beside it. The Indians sold valuable furs for scanty payment in blankets, beads, muskets, and intoxicating drinks. The prudent Dutchmen grew rich, and were becoming numerous. But a fierce and prolonged war with the Indians broke out. The Dutch, having taken offence at something done by the savages, expressed their wrath by the massacre of an entire tribe. All the Indians of that region made common cause against the dangerous strangers. All the Dutch villages were burned down.

1609 A.D.

1643 A.D.

Long Island became a desert. The Dutchmen were driven in to the southern tip of the island on which New York stands. They ran a palisade across the island in the line of what is now Wall Street. To-day, Wall Street is the scene of the largest monetary transactions ever known among men. The hot fever of speculation rages there incessantly, with a fury unknown elsewhere. But then, it was the line within which a disheartened and diminishing band of colonists strove to maintain themselves against a savage foe.

The war came to an end as wars even then required to do.

1645 A.D. For twenty years the colony continued to flourish under the government of a sagacious Dutchman called Petrus Stuyvesant. Petrus had been a soldier, and had lost a leg in the wars. He was a brave and true-hearted man, but withal despotic. When his subjects petitioned for some part in the making of laws, he was astonished at their boldness. He took it upon him to inspect the merchants' books. He persecuted the Lutherans and "the abominable sect of Quakers."

It cannot be said that his government was faultless. The colony prospered under it, however, and a continued emigration from Europe increased its importance. But in the twentieth year, certain English ships of war sailed up the bay, and, without a word of explanation, anchored near the settlement. Governor Petrus was from home, but they sent for him, and he came with speed. He hastened to the fort and looked out into the bay. There lay the ships—grim, silent, ominously near. Appalled by the presence of his unexpected visitors, the Governor sent to ask wherefore they had come. His alarm was well founded. For Charles II. of England had presented to his brother James of York a vast stretch of territory, including the region which the Dutch had chosen for their settlement. It was not his to give, but that signified nothing either to Charles or to James. These ships had come to take possession in the Duke of York's name. A good many of the colonists were English, and they were well pleased to be under their own Government. They would not fight. The Dutch remembered the Governor's tyrannies, and they would not fight. Governor Petrus was prepared to fight single-handed. He had the twenty guns of the fort loaded, and was resolute to fire upon the ships. So at least he professed. But the inhabitants begged him, in mercy to them, to forbear; and he suffered himself to be led by two clergymen away from the loaded guns. It was alleged, to his disparagement, afterwards, that he had "allowed himself to be persuaded by ministers and other chicken-hearted persons." Be that as it may, King Charles's errand was done. The little town of 1500 inhabitants, with all the neighbouring settlements, passed quietly under English rule. And the future Empire City was named New York, in honour of one of the meanest tyrants who ever disgraced the English throne. With the settlements on the Hudson there fell also into the hands of the English those of New Jersey, which the Dutch had conquered from the Swedes.

IX.

PENNSYLVANIA.

It was not till the year 1682 that the uneventful but quietly prosperous career of Pennsylvania began. The Stuarts were again upon the throne of England. They had learned nothing from their exile; and now, with the hour of their final rejection at hand, they were as wickedly despotic as ever.

William Penn was the son of an admiral who had gained victories for England, and enjoyed the favour of the royal family as well as of the eminent statesmen of his time. The highest honours of the State would in due time have come within the young man's reach, and the brightest hopes of his future were reasonably entertained by his friends. To the dismay of all, Penn became a Quaker. It was an unspeakable humiliation to the well-connected admiral. He turned his son out of doors, trusting that hunger would subdue his intractable spirit. After a time, however, he relented, and the youthful heretic was restored to favour. His father's influence could not shield him from persecution. Penn had suffered fine, and had lain in the Tower for his opinions.

Ere long the admiral died, and Penn succeeded to his possessions. It deeply grieved him that his brethren in the faith should endure such wrongs as were continually inflicted upon them. He could do nothing at home to mitigate the severities under which they groaned. Therefore he formed the great design of leading them forth to a new world. King

Charles owed to the admiral a sum of £16,000, and this doubtful investment had descended from the father to the son. Penn offered to take payment in land, and the King readily bestowed upon him a vast region stretching westward from the river Delaware. Here Penn proposed to found a State free and self-governing. It was his noble ambition "to show men as free and as happy as they can be." He proclaimed to the people already settled in his new dominions that they should be governed by laws of their own making. "Whatever sober and free men can reasonably desire," he told them, "for the security and improvement of their own happiness, I shall heartily comply with." He was as good as his word. The people appointed representatives, by whom a Constitution was framed. Penn confirmed the arrangements which the people chose to adopt.

Penn dealt justly and kindly with the Indians, and they requited him with a reverential love such as they evinced to no other Englishman. The neighbouring colonies waged bloody wars with the Indians who lived around them—now inflicting defeats which were almost exterminating—now sustaining hideous massacres. Penn's Indians were his children and most loyal subjects. No drop of Quaker blood was ever shed by Indian hand in the Pennsylvanian territory. Soon after Penn's arrival, he invited the chief men of the Indian tribes to a conference. The meeting took place beneath a huge elm-tree. The pathless forest has long given way to the houses and streets of Philadelphia, but a marble monument points out to strangers the scene of this memorable interview. Penn, with a few companions, unarmed, and dressed according to the simple fashion of their sect, met the crowd of formidable savages. They met, he assured them, as brothers "on the broad pathway of good faith and good will." No advantage was to be taken on either side. All was to be "openness and love;" and Penn meant what he said. Strong in the power of truth and kindness, he bent the fierce savages of the Delaware to his will. They vowed "to live in love with William Penn and his children as long as the moon and the sun shall endure." They kept their vow. Long years after, they were known to recount to strangers, with deep emotion, the words which Penn had spoken to them under the old elm-tree of Shakamaxon.

The fame of Penn's settlement went abroad in all lands. Men wearied with the vulgar tyranny of Kings heard gladly that the reign of freedom and tranquillity was established on the banks of the Delaware. An asylum was opened "for the good and oppressed of every nation." Of these there was no lack. Pennsylvania had nothing to attract such "dissolute persons" as had laid the foundations of Virginia. But grave and God-fearing men from all the Protestant countries sought a home where they might live as conscience taught them. The new colony grew apace. Its natural advantages were tempting. Penn reported it as "a good land, with plentiful springs, the air clear and fresh, and an innumerable quantity of wild-fowl and fish; what Abraham, Isaac, and Jacob would be well-contented with." During the first year, twenty-two vessels arrived, bringing two thousand persons. In three years, Philadelphia was a town of six hundred houses. It was half a century from its foundation before New York attained equal dimensions.

When Penn, after a few years, revisited England, he was able truly to relate that "things went on sweetly with Friends in Pennsylvania; that they increased finely in outward things and in wisdom."

X.

GEORGIA.

THE thirteen States which composed the original Union were Virginia, Massachusetts, Connecticut, Rhode Island, New Hampshire, Delaware, Maryland, Pennsylvania, New York, New Jersey, North Carolina, South Carolina, and Georgia.

Of these the latest born was Georgia. Only fifty years had passed since Penn established the Quaker State on the banks of the Delaware. But changes greater than centuries have sometimes wrought had taken place. The Revolution had vindicated the liberties of the British people. The tyrant House of Stuart had been cast out, and with its fall the era of despotic government had closed. The real governing power was no longer the King, but the Parliament.

<small>1732 A.D.</small>

Among the members of Parliament during the rule of Sir Robert Walpole was one almost unknown to us now, but deserving of honour beyond most men of his time. His name was James Oglethorpe. He was a soldier, and had fought against the Turks and in the great Marlborough wars against Louis the Fourteenth. In advanced life he became the friend of Samuel Johnson. Dr. Johnson urged him to write some account of his adventures. "I know no one," he said, "whose life would be more interesting: if I were furnished with materials I should be very glad to write it." Edmund Burke considered him "a more extraordinary person than any he had ever read of."

John Wesley "blessed God that ever he was born." Oglethorpe attained the great age of ninety-six, and died in the year 1785. The year before his death he attended the sale of Dr. Johnson's books, and was there met by Samuel Rogers the poet. "Even then," says Rogers, "he was the finest figure of a man you ever saw, but very, very old; the flesh of his face like parchment."

In Oglethorpe's time it was in the power of a creditor to imprison, according to his pleasure, the man who owed him money and was not able to pay it. It was a common circumstance that a man should be imprisoned during a long series of years for a trifling debt. Oglethorpe had a friend upon whom this hard fate had fallen. His attention was thus painfully called to the cruelties which were inflicted upon the unfortunate and helpless. He appealed to Parliament, and after inquiry a partial remedy was obtained. The benevolent exertions of Oglethorpe procured liberty for multitudes who but for him might have ended their lives in captivity.

This, however, did not content him. Liberty was an incomplete gift to men who had lost, or perhaps had scarcely ever possessed, the faculty of earning their own maintenance. Oglethorpe devised how he might carry these unfortunates to a new world, where, under happier auspices, they might open a fresh career. He obtained from King George II. a charter by which the country between the Savannah and the Alatamaha, and stretching westward to the Pacific, was erected into the province of Georgia. It was to be a refuge for the deserving poor, and next to them for Protestants suffering persecution. Parliament voted £10,000 in aid of the humane enterprise, and many benevolent persons were liberal with their gifts. In November the first exodus of the insolvent took place. Oglethorpe sailed with one hundred and twenty emigrants, mainly selected from the prisons—penniless, but of good repute. He surveyed the coasts of Georgia, and chose a site for the capital of

1732
A.D.

his new State. He pitched his tent where Savannah now stands, and at once proceeded to mark out the line of streets and squares.

Next year the colony was joined by about a hundred German Protestants, who were then under persecution for their beliefs. The colonists received this addition to their numbers with joy. A place of residence had been chosen for them which the devout and thankful strangers named Ebenezer. They were charmed with their new abode. The river and the hills, they said, reminded them of home. They applied themselves with steady industry to the cultivation of indigo and silk; and they prospered.

The fame of Oglethorpe's enterprise spread over Europe. All struggling men against whom the battle of life went hard looked to Georgia as a land of promise. They were the men who most urgently required to emigrate; but they were not always the men best fitted to conquer the difficulties of the immigrant's life. The progress of the colony was slow. The poor persons of whom it was originally composed were honest but ineffective, and could not in Georgia more than in England find out the way to become self-supporting. Encouragements were given which drew from Germany, from Switzerland, and from the Highlands of Scotland, men of firmer texture of mind—better fitted to subdue the wilderness and bring forth its treasures.

With Oglethorpe there went out, on his second expedition to Georgia, the two brothers John and Charles Wesley. Charles went as secretary to the Governor. John was even then, although a very young man, a preacher of unusual promise. He burned to spread the gospel among the settlers and their Indian neighbours. He spent two years in Georgia, and these were unsuccessful years. His character was unformed; his zeal out of proportion to his discretion. The people felt that he preached "personal satires" at them. He involved himself in quarrels, and at last had to leave the

1736 A.D.

colony secretly, fearing arrest at the instance of some whom he had offended. He returned to begin his great career in England, with the feeling that his residence in Georgia had been of much value to himself, but of very little to the people whom he sought to benefit.

Just as Wesley reached England, his fellow-labourer George Whitefield sailed for Georgia. There were now little settlements spreading inland, and Whitefield visited these—bearing to them the word of life. He founded an Orphan-House at Savannah, and supported it by contributions—obtained easily from men under the power of his unequalled eloquence. He visited Georgia very frequently, and his love for that colony remained with him to the last.

Slavery was, at the outset, forbidden in Georgia. It was opposed to the gospel, Oglethorpe said, and therefore not to be allowed. He foresaw, besides, what has been so bitterly experienced since, that slavery must degrade the poor white labourer. But soon a desire sprung up among the less scrupulous of the settlers to have the use of slaves. Within seven years from the first landing, slave-ships were discharging their cargoes at Savannah.

XI.

SLAVERY.

In the month of December 1620, the Pilgrim Fathers landed from the *Mayflower*. Their landing takes rank among our great historical transactions. The rock which first received their footsteps is a sacred spot, to which the citizens of great and powerful States make reverential pilgrimages. And right it should be so. For the vast influence for good which New England exerts, and must ever exert, in the world's affairs, has risen upon the foundation laid by these sickly and storm-wearied Pilgrims.

A few months previously another landing had taken place, destined in the fulness of time to bear the strangest of fruits. In the month of August a Dutch ship of war sailed up the James river and put twenty negroes ashore upon the Virginian coast. It was a wholly unnoticed proceeding. No name or lineage had these sable strangers. No one cared to know from what tribe they sprang, or how it fared with them in their sorrowful journeying. Yet these men were Pilgrim Fathers too. They were the first negro slaves in a land whose history, during the next century and a half, was to receive a dark, and finally a bloody, colouring from the fact of Negro Slavery.

The negro slave trade was an early result of the discovery of America. To utilize the vast possessions which Columbus had bestowed upon her, Spain deemed that compulsory labour was indispensable. The natives of the country naturally fell the first victims to this necessity. Terrible desolations were wrought among the poor Indians. Proud and melancholy, they could not be reconciled to their bondage. They perished by thousands under the merciless hand of their new task-masters.

Charles V. heard with remorse of this ruin of the native races. Indian slavery was at once and peremptorily forbidden. But labourers must be obtained, or those splendid possessions would relapse into wilderness. Spanish merchants traded to the coasts of Africa, where they bought gold dust and ivory for beads and ribands and scarlet cloaks. They found there a harmless idle people, whose simple wants were supplied without effort on their part, and who, in the absence of inducement, neither laboured nor fought. The Spaniards bethought them of these men to cultivate their fields, to labour in their mines. They were gentle and tractable; they were heathens, and therefore the proper inheritance of good Catholics; by baptism and instruction in the faith their souls would be saved from destruction. Motives of the most diverse kinds urged the introduction of the negro. At first the traffic extended no further than to criminals. Thieves and murderers, who must otherwise have been put to death, enriched their chiefs by the purchase-money which the Spaniards were eager to pay. But on all that coast no rigour of law could produce offenders in numbers sufficient to meet the demand. Soon the limitation ceased. Unoffending persons were systematically kidnapped and sold. The tribes went to war, in the hope of taking prisoners whom they might dispose of to the Spaniards.

1542 A.D.

England was not engaged in that traffic at its outset. Ere long her hands were as deeply tainted with its guilt as those of any other country. But for a time her intercourse with Africa was for blameless purposes of commerce. And while that continued the English were regarded with confidence by the Africans. At length one John Lok, a shipmaster, stole five black men and brought them to London. The next Englishman who visited Africa found that that theft had damaged the good name of his countrymen. His voyage was unprofitable, for the natives feared him. When this was told in London the mercantile world was troubled, for the African trade was a gainful one. The five stolen men were conveyed safely home again. **1557 A.D.**

This was the opening of our African slave-trade. Then, for the first time, did our fathers feel the dark temptation, and thus hesitatingly did they at first yield to its power. The traffic in gold dust and ivory continued. Every Englishman who visited the African coast had occasion to know how actively and how profitably Spain, and Portugal too, traded in slaves. He knew that on all that rich coast there was no merchandise so lucrative as the unfortunate people themselves. It was not an age when such seductions could be long withstood. The English traders of that day were not the men to be held back from a gainful traffic by mere considerations of humanity.

Sir John Hawkins made the first English venture in slave-trading. He sailed with three vessels to Sierra Leone. There, by purchase or by violence, he possessed himself of three hundred negroes. With this freight he crossed the Atlantic, and at St. Domingo he sold the whole to a great profit. The fame of his gains caused sensation in England. He was encouraged to undertake a second expedition. Queen Elizabeth and many of her courtiers took shares in the venture. After many difficulties, Hawkins collected five hundred negroes. His voyage was a troublous one. He was beset with calms. Water ran short, and it was feared that a portion of the cargo must have been flung overboard. "Almighty God, however," says this devout man-stealer, "who never suffers his **1562 A.D.**

elect to perish," brought him to the West Indies without loss of a man. But there had arrived before him a rigorous interdict from the King of Spain against the admission of foreign vessels to any of his West Indian ports. Hawkins was too stouthearted to suffer such frustration of his enterprise. After some useless negotiation, he landed a hundred men with two pieces of cannon; landed and sold his negroes; paid the tax which he himself had fixed; and soon in quiet England divided his gains with his royal and noble patrons. Thus was the slave-trade established in England. Three centuries after, we look with horror and remorse upon the results which have followed.

In most of the colonies there was unquestionably a desire for the introduction of the negro. But ere many years the colonists became aware that they were rapidly involving themselves in grave difficulties. The increase of the coloured population alarmed them. Heavy debts, incurred for the purchase of slaves, disordered their finances. The production of tobacco, indigo, and other articles of Southern growth, exceeded the demand, and prices fell ruinously low. There were occasionally proposals made—although not very favourably entertained—with a view to emancipation. But the opposition of the colonists to the African slave-trade was very decided. Very frequent attempts to limit the traffic were made even in the Southern colonies, where slave labour was most valuable. Soon after the

1787 A.D.
Revolution, several Slave-owning States prohibited the importation of slaves. The Constitution provided that Congress might suppress the slave-trade after the lapse of twenty years. But for the resistance of South Carolina and Georgia the prohibition would have been immediate. And at length, at the earliest moment when it was possible, Con-

1807 A.D.
gress gave effect to the general sentiment by enacting "that no slaves be imported into any of the thirteen United Colonies."

And why had this not been done earlier? If the colonists were sincere in their desire to suppress this base traffic, why did they not suppress it? The reason is not difficult to find. England would not permit them. England forced the slave-trade upon the reluctant colonists. The English Parliament watched with paternal care over the interests of this hideous traffic. During the first half of the eighteenth century Parliament was continually legislating to this effect. Every restraint upon the largest development of the trade was removed with scrupulous care. Everything that diplomacy could do to open new markets was done. When the colonists sought by imposing a tax to check the importation of slaves, that tax was repealed. Land was given free, in the West Indies, on condition that the settler should keep four negroes for every hundred acres. Forts were built on the African coast for the protection of the trade. So recently as the year 1749 an Act was passed bestowing additional encouragements upon slave-traders, and emphatically asserting "the slave-trade is very advantageous to Great Britain." There are no passages in all our history so humiliating as these.

It is marvellous that such things were done—deliberately, and with all the solemnities of legal sanction—by men not unacquainted with the Christian religion, and humane in all the ordinary relations of life. The Popish Inquisition inflicted no suffering more barbarously cruel than was endured by the victim of the slave-trader. Hundreds of men and women, with chains upon their limbs, were packed closely together into the holds of small vessels. There, during weeks of suffering, they remained, enduring fierce tropical heat, often deprived of water and of food. They were all young and strong, for the fastidious slave-trader rejected men over thirty as uselessly old. But the strength of the strongest sunk under the horrors of this voyage. Often it happened that the greater portion of the cargo had to be flung overboard. Under the most favourable circumstances, it was expected that one slave in every five would perish. In every cargo of five hundred, one hundred would suffer a miserable death. And the public sentiment of England fully sanctioned a traffic of which these horrors were a necessary part.

At one time the idea was prevalent in the colonies that it was contrary to Scripture to hold a baptized person in slavery. The colonists did not on that account liberate their slaves. They escaped the difficulty in the opposite direction. They withheld baptism and religious instruction. England took some pains to put them right on this question. The Bishops of the Church and the law-officers of the Crown issued authoritative declarations, asserting the entire lawfulness of owning Christians. The colonial legislatures followed with enactments to the same effect. The colonists, thus reassured, gave consent that the souls of their unhappy dependants should be cared for.

Up to the Revolution it was estimated that 300,000 negroes had been brought into the country direct from Africa. The entire coloured population was supposed to amount to nearly half a million.

XII.

EARLY GOVERNMENT.

There was at the outset considerable diversity of pattern among the governments of the colonies. As time wore on, the diversity lessened, and one great type becomes visible in all. There is a Governor appointed by the King. There is a Parliament chosen by the people. Parliament holds the purse-strings. The Governor applies for what moneys the public service seems to him to require. Parliament, as a rule, grants his demands, but not without consideration, and a distinct assertion of its right to refuse should cause appear. As the Revolution drew near, the function of the Governor became gradually circumscribed by the pressure of the Assemblies. When the Governor, as representing the King, fell into variance with the popular will, the representatives of the people assumed the whole business of Government. The most loyal of the colonies resolutely defied the encroachments of the King or his Governor. They had a pleasure and a pride in their connection with England; but they were at the same time essentially a self-governing people. From the government which existed before the Revolution it was easy for them to step into a federal union. The colonists had all their interests and all their grievances in common. It was natural for them, when trouble arose, to appoint representatives who should deliberate regarding their affairs. These representatives required an Executive to give practical effect to their resolutions. The officer who was appointed for that purpose was called, not King, but President; and was chosen, not for life, but for four years. By this simple and natural process arose the American Government.

At first Virginia was governed by two Councils, one of which was English and the other Colonial. Both were entirely under the King's control. In a very few years the representative system was introduced, and a popular assembly, over whose proceedings the Governor retained the right of veto, regulated the affairs of the colony. Virginia was the least democratic of the colonies. Her leanings were always towards monarchy. She maintained her loyalty to the Stuarts. Charles II. ruled her in his exile, and was crowned in a robe of Virginian silk, presented by the devoted colonists. The baffled Cavaliers sought refuge in Virginia from the hateful triumph of Republicanism. Virginia refused to acknowledge the Commonwealth, and had to be subjected by force. When the exiled House was restored, her joy knew no bounds.

The New England States were of different temper and different government. While yet on board the *Mayflower*, the Pilgrims, as we have seen, formed themselves into a body politic, elected their Governor, and bound themselves to submit to his authority, "confiding in his prudence that he would not adventure upon any matter of moment without consent of the rest." Every church member was an elector. For sixty years this democratic form of government was continued, till the despotic James II. overturned it in the closing years of his unhappy reign. The Pilgrims carried with them from England a bitter feeling of the wrongs which Kings had inflicted on them, and they arrived in America a people fully disposed to govern themselves. They cordially supported Cromwell. Cromwell, on his part, so highly esteemed the people of New England, that he invited them to return to Europe, and offered them settlements in Ireland. They delayed for two years to proclaim Charles II. when he was restored to the English throne. They sheltered the regicides who fled from the King's vengeance. They hailed the Revolution, by which the Stuarts were expelled and constitutional monarchy set up in England. Of all the American colonies, those of New England were the most democratic, and the most intolerant of royal interference with their liberties.

New York was bestowed upon the Duke of York, who for a time appointed the Governor. Pennsylvania was a grant to Penn, who exercised the same authority. Ultimately, however, in all cases, the appointment of Governor rested with the King, while the representatives were chosen by the people.

BOOK II.

I.

GEORGE WASHINGTON.

In the year 1740 there fell out a great European war. There was some doubt who should fill the Austrian throne. The Emperor had just died, leaving no son or brother to inherit his dignities. His daughter, Maria Theresa, stepped into her father's place, and soon made it apparent that she was strong enough to maintain what she had done. Two or three Kings thought they had a better right than she to the throne. The other Kings ranged themselves on this side or on that. The idea of looking on while foolish neighbours destroyed themselves by senseless war, had not yet been suggested. Every King took part in a great war, and sent his people forth to slay and be slain, quite as a matter of course. So they raised great armies, fought great battles, burned cities, wasted countries, inflicted and endured unutterable miseries, all to settle the question about this lady's throne. But the lady was of a heroic spirit, well worthy to govern, and she held her own, and lived and died an Empress.

During these busy years, a Virginian mother, widowed in early life, was training up her eldest son in the fear of God—all unaware, as she infused the love of goodness and duty into his mind, that she was giving a colour to the history of her country throughout all its coming ages. That boy's name was George Washington. He was born in 1732. His father —a gentleman of good fortune, with a pedigree which can be traced beyond the Norman Conquest—died when his son was eleven years of age. Upon George's mother devolved the care of his upbringing. She was a devout woman, of excellent sense and deep affections; but a strict disciplinarian, and of a temper which could brook no shadow of insubordination. Under her rule—gentle, and yet strong—George learned obedience and self-control. In boyhood he gave remarkable promise of those excellences which distinguished his mature years. His schoolmates recognized the calm judicial character of his mind, and he became in all their disputes the arbiter from whose decision there was no appeal. He inherited his mother's love of command, happily tempered by a lofty disinterestedness and a love of justice, which seemed to render it impossible that he should do or permit aught that was unfair. His person was large and powerful. His face expressed the thoughtfulness and serene strength of his character. He excelled in all athletic exercises. His youthful delight in such pursuits developed his physical capabilities to the utmost, and gave him endurance to bear the hardships which lay before him.

Young gentlemen of Virginia were not educated then so liberally as they have been since. It was presumed that Washington would be a mere Virginian proprietor and farmer, as his father had been; and his education was no higher than that position then demanded. He never learned any language but his own. The teacher of his early years was also the sexton of the parish. And even when he was taken to an institution of a more advanced description, he attempted no higher study than the keeping of accounts and the copying of legal and mercantile papers. A few years later, it was thought he might enter the civil or military service of his country; and he was put to the study of mathematics and land-surveying.

George Washington did nothing by halves. In youth, as in manhood, he did thoroughly what he had to do. His school exercise-books are models of neatness and accuracy. His plans and measurements made while he studied land-surveying were as scrupulously exact as if great pecuniary interests depended upon them. In his eighteenth year he was employed by Government as surveyor of public lands. Many of his surveys were recorded in the county offices, and remain to this day. Long experience has established their unvarying accuracy. In all disputes to which they have any relevancy, their evidence is accepted as decisive. During the years which preceded the Revolution he managed his estates, packed and shipped his own tobacco and flour, kept his own books, conducted his own correspondence. His books may still be seen. Perhaps no clearer or more accurate record of business transactions has been kept in America since the Father of American Independence rested from book-keeping. The flour which he shipped to foreign ports came to be known as his, and the Washington brand was habitually exempted from inspection. A most reliable man; his words and his deeds, his professions and his practice, are ever found in most perfect harmony. By some he has been regarded as a stolid, prosaic person, wanting in those features of character which captivate the minds of men. Not so. In an earlier age George Washington would have been a true knight-errant with an insatiable thirst for adventure and a passionate love of battle. He had in high degree those qualities which make ancient knighthood picturesque. But higher qualities than these bore rule within him. He had wisdom beyond most, giving him deep insight into the wants of his time. He had clear perceptions of the duty which lay to his hand. What he saw to be right, the strongest impulses of his soul constrained him to do. A massive intellect and an iron strength of will were given to him, with a gentle, loving heart, with dauntless courage, with purity and loftiness of aim. He had a work of extraordinary difficulty to perform. History rejoices to recognize in him a revolutionary leader against whom no questionable transaction has ever been alleged.

The history of America presents, in one important feature, a very striking contrast to the history of nearly all older countries. In the old countries, history gathers round some one grand central figure—some judge, or priest, or king—whose biography tells all that has to be told concerning the time in which he lived. That one predominating person—David, Alexander, Cæsar, Napoleon—is among his people what the sun is in the planetary system. All movement originates and terminates in him, and the history of the people is merely a record of what he has chosen to do or caused to be done. In America it has not been so. The American system leaves no room for predominating persons. It affords none of those exhibitions of solitary, all-absorbing grandeur which are so picturesque, and have been so pernicious. Her history is a history of her people, and of no conspicuous individuals. Once only in her career is it otherwise. During the lifetime of George Washington her history clings very closely to him; and the biography of her great chief becomes in a very unusual degree the history of the country.

II.

BENJAMIN FRANKLIN.

WHILE Washington's boyhood was being passed on the banks of the Potomac, a young man, destined to help him in gaining the independence of the country, was toiling hard in the city of Philadelphia to earn an honest livelihood. His name was Benjamin Franklin. He kept a small stationer's shop. He edited a newspaper. He was a bookbinder. He made ink. He sold rags, soap, and coffee. He was also a printer, employing a journeyman and an apprentice to aid him in his labours. He was a thriving man; but he was not ashamed to convey along the streets, in a wheelbarrow, the paper which he bought for the purposes of his trade. As a boy he had been studious and thoughtful. As a man he was prudent, sagacious, trustworthy. His prudence was, however, somewhat low-toned and earthly. He loved and sought to marry a deserving young woman, who returned his affection. There was in those days a debt of one hundred pounds upon his printing-house. He demanded that the father of the young lady should pay off this debt. The father was unable to do so. Whereupon the worldly Benjamin decisively broke off the contemplated alliance.

When he had earned a moderate competency he ceased to labour at his business. Henceforth he laboured to serve his fellow-men. Philadelphia owes to Franklin her university, her hospital, her fire-brigade, her first and greatest library.

He earned renown as a man of science. It had long been his thought that lightning and electricity were the same; but he found no way to prove the truth of his theory. At length he made a kite fitted suitably for his experiment. He stole away from his house during a thunder-storm, having told no one but his son, who accompanied him. The kite was sent up among the stormy clouds, and the anxious philosopher waited. For a time no response to his eager questioning was granted, and Franklin's countenance fell. But at length he felt the welcome shock, and his heart thrilled with the high consciousness that he had added to the sum of human knowledge. 1752 A.D.

When the troubles arose in connection with the Stamp Act, Franklin was sent to England to defend the rights of the colonists. The vigour of his intellect, the matured wisdom of his opinions, gained for him a wonderful supremacy over the men with whom he was brought into contact. He was examined before Parliament. Edmund Burke said that the scene reminded him of a master examined by a parcel of school-boys, so conspicuously was the witness superior to his interrogators. 1766 A.D.

Franklin was an early advocate of independence, and aided in preparing the famous Declaration. In all the councils of that eventful time he bore a leading part. He was the first American Ambassador to France; and the good sense and vivacity of the old printer gained for him high favour in the fashionable world of Paris. He lived to aid in framing the Constitution under which America has enjoyed prosperity so great. Soon after he passed away. A few months before his death he wrote to Washington :—" I am now finishing my eighty-fourth year, and probably with it my career in this life; but in whatever state of existence I am placed hereafter, if I retain any memory of what has passed here, I shall with it retain the esteem, respect, and affection with which I have long regarded you." 1777 A.D. 1789 A.D.

III.

THE VALLEY OF THE OHIO.

1748
A.D.
THE peace of Aix-la-Chapelle, which gave a brief repose to Europe, left unsettled the contending claims of France and England upon American territory. France had possessions in Canada and also in Louisiana, at the extreme south, many hundreds of miles away. She claimed the entire line of the Mississippi river, with its tributaries; and she had given effect to her pretensions by erecting forts at intervals to connect her settlements in the north with those in the south. Her claim included the Valley of the Ohio. This was a vast and fertile region, whose value had just been discovered by the English. It was yet unpeopled; but its vegetation gave evidence of wealth unknown to the colonists in the eastern settlements. The French, to establish their claim, sent three hundred soldiers into the valley, and nailed upon the trees leaden plates which bore the royal arms of France. They strove by gifts and persuasion to gain over the natives, and expelled the English traders who had made their adventurous way into those recesses. The English, on their part, were not idle. A great trading company was formed, which, in return for certain grants of land, became bound to colonize the valley, to establish trading relations with the Indians, and to maintain a competent military force. This was in the year 1749. In that age there was but one solution of such difficulties. Governments had not learned to reason. They could only fight. Early

in 1751 both parties were actively preparing for war. That war went ill with France. When the sword was sheathed in 1759, she had lost not only Ohio, but the whole of Canada.

When the fighting began it was conducted on the English side wholly by the colonists. Virginia raised a little army. Washington, then a lad of twenty-one, was offered the command, so great was the confidence already felt in his capacity. It was war in miniature as yet. The object of Washington in the campaign was to reach a certain fort on the Ohio, and hold it as a barrier against French encroachment. He had his artillery to carry with him, and to render that possible he had to make a road through the wilderness. He struggled heroically with the difficulties of his position. But he could not advance at any better speed than two miles a-day; and he was not destined to reach the fort on the Ohio. After toiling on as he best might for six weeks, he learned that the French were seeking him with a force far outnumbering his. He halted, and hastily constructed a rude intrenchment, which he called Fort Necessity, because his men had nearly starved while they worked at it. He had three hundred Virginians with him, and some Indians. The Indians deserted so soon as occasion arose for their services. The French attack was not long withheld. Early one summer morning a sentinel came in bleeding from a French bullet. All that day the fight lasted. At night the French summoned Washington to surrender. The garrison were to march out with flag and drum, leaving only their artillery. Washington could do no better, and he surrendered. Thus ended the first campaign in the war which was to drive France from Ohio and Canada. Thus opened the military career of the man who was to drive England from the noblest of her colonial possessions.

1754
A.D.

But now the English Government awoke to the necessity of vigorous measures to rescue the endangered Valley of the Ohio.

A campaign was planned which was to expel the French from Ohio, and wrest from them some portions of their Canadian territory. The execution of this great design was intrusted to General Braddock, with a force which it was deemed would overbear all resistance. Braddock was a veteran who had seen the wars of forty years. Among the fields on which he had gained his knowledge of war was Culloden, where he had borne a part in trampling out the rebellion of the Scotch. He was a brave and experienced soldier, and a likely man, it was thought, to do the work assigned to him. But that proved a sad miscalculation. Braddock had learned the rules of war; but he had no capacity to comprehend its principles. In the pathless forests of America he could do nothing better than strive to give literal effect to those maxims which he had found applicable in the well-trodden battle-grounds of Europe.

The failure of Washington in his first campaign had not deprived him of public confidence. Braddock heard such accounts of his efficiency that he invited him to join his staff. Washington, eager to efface the memory of his defeat, gladly accepted the offer.

1755
A.D.

The troops disembarked at Alexandria. The colonists, little used to the presence of regular soldiers, were greatly emboldened by their splendid aspect and faultless discipline, and felt that the hour of final triumph was at hand. After some delay, the army, with such reinforcements as the province afforded, began its march. Braddock's object was to reach Fort Du Quesne, the great centre of French influence on the Ohio. It was this same fort of which Washington endeavoured so manfully to possess himself in his disastrous campaign of last year.

Fort Du Quesne had been built by the English, and taken from them by the French. It stood at the confluence of the Alleghany and Monongahela; which rivers, by their union at this point, form the Ohio. It was a rude piece of fortification, but the circumstances admitted of no better. The fort was built of the trunks of trees. Wooden huts for the soldiers surrounded it. A little space had been cleared in the forest, and a few patches of wheat and Indian corn grew luxuriantly in that rich soil. The unbroken forest stretched all around. Three years later the little fort was retaken by the English, and named Fort Pitt. Then in time it grew to be a town, and was called Pittsburg. And men found in its neighbourhood boundless wealth of iron and of coal. To-day a great and fast-growing city stands where, a century ago, the rugged fort with its cluster of rugged huts were the sole occupants. And the rivers, then so lonely, are ploughed by innumerable keels; and the air is dark with the smoke of innumerable furnaces. The judgment of the sagacious Englishmen who deemed this a locality which they would do well to get hold of, has been amply borne out by the experience of posterity.

Braddock had no doubt that the fort would yield to him directly he showed himself before it. Benjamin Franklin looked at the project with his shrewd, cynical eye. He told Braddock that he would assuredly take the fort if he could only reach it; but that the long slender line which his army must form in its march "would be cut like thread into several pieces" by the hostile Indians. Braddock "smiled at his ignorance." Benjamin offered no further opinion. It was his duty to collect horses and carriages for the use of the expedition, and he did what was required of him in silence.

The expedition crept slowly forward, never achieving more than three or four miles in a day; stopping, as Washington said, "to level every mole-hill, to erect a bridge over every brook." It left Alexandria on the 20th April. On the 9th July Braddock, with half his army, was near the fort. There was yet no evidence that resistance was intended. No enemy had been seen. The troops marched on as to assured victory. So confident was their chief, that he refused to employ scouts, and did not deign to inquire what enemy might be lurking near.

The march was along a road twelve feet wide, in a ravine, with high ground in front and on both sides. Suddenly the Indian war-whoop burst from the woods. A murderous fire smote down the troops. The provincials, not unused to this description of warfare, sheltered themselves behind trees and fought with steady courage. Braddock, clinging to his old rules, strove to maintain his order of battle on the open ground. A carnage, most grim and lamentable, was the result. His undefended soldiers were shot down by an unseen foe. For three hours the struggle lasted. Then the men broke and fled in utter rout and panic. Braddock, vainly fighting, fell mortally wounded. He was carried off the field by some of his soldiers. The poor pedantic man never got over his astonishment at a defeat so inconsistent with the established rules of war. "Who would have thought it?" he murmured, as they bore him from the field. He scarcely spoke again, and died in two or three days. Nearly eight hundred men, killed and wounded, were lost in this disastrous encounter—about one-half of the entire force engaged.

All the while England and France were nominally at peace. But now war was declared. The other European powers fell into their accustomed places in the strife, and the flames of war spread far and wide. On land and on sea the European people strove to shed blood and destroy property, and thus produce human misery to the largest possible extent. At the outset every fight brought defeat and shame to England. English armies under incapable leaders were sent out to America and ignominiously routed by the French. On the continent of Europe the uniform course of disaster was scarcely broken by a single victory. Even at sea, England seemed to have fallen from her high estate, and her fleets turned back from the presence of an enemy.

The rage of the people knew no bounds. The admiral who had not fought the enemy when he should have done so, was hanged. The Prime Minister began to tremble for his neck. One or two disasters more, and the public indignation might demand a greater victim than an unfortunate admiral. The Ministry resigned, and William Pitt, afterwards Earl of Chatham, came into power.

And then, all at once, the scene changed, and there began a career of triumph more brilliant than even England had ever known. The French fleets were destroyed. French possessions all over the world were seized. French armies were defeated. Every post brought news of victory. For once the English people, greedy as they are of military glory, were satisfied.

One of the most splendid successes of Pitt's administration was gained in America. The colonists had begun to lose respect for the English Army and the English Government. But Pitt quickly regained their confidence. They raised an army of 50,000 men to help his schemes for the extinction of French power. A strong English force was sent out, and a formidable invasion of Canada was organized. **1759 A.D.**

Most prominent among the strong points held by the French was the city of Quebec. Thither in the month of June came a powerful English fleet, with an army under the command of General Wolfe. Captain James Cook, the famous navigator, who discovered so many of the sunny islands of the Pacific, was master of one of the ships. Quebec stands upon a peninsula formed by the junction of the St. Charles and the St. Lawrence rivers. The lower town was upon the beach. The upper was on the cliffs, which at that point rise precipitously to a height of two hundred feet. Wolfe tried the effect of a bombardment. He laid the lower town in ruins very easily, but the upper town was too remote from his batteries to sustain much injury. It seemed as if the enterprise would prove too much for the English, and the sensitive Wolfe was thrown by disappointment and anxiety into a violent fever. But he was not the man to be baffled. The shore for miles above the town was carefully searched. An opening was found whence a path wound up the cliff. Here Wolfe would land his men, and lead them to the Heights of Abraham. Once there, they would defeat the French and take Quebec, or die where they stood.

On a starlight night in September the soldiers were embarked in boats which dropped down the river to the chosen landing-place. As the boat which carried Wolfe floated silently down, he recited to his officers Gray's "Elegy in a Country Church-yard," then newly received from England; and he exclaimed at its close, "I would rather be the author of that poem than take Quebec to-morrow." He was a man of feeble bodily frame, but he wielded the power which genius in its higher forms confers. Amid the excitements of impending battle he could walk, with the old delight, in the quiet paths of literature.

The soldiers landed and clambered, as they best might, up the rugged pathway. All through the night armed men stepped silently from the boats and silently scaled those formidable cliffs. The sailors contrived to drag up a few guns. When morning came, the whole army stood upon the Heights of Abraham ready for the battle.

Montcalm, the French commander, was so utterly taken by surprise that he refused at first to believe the presence of the English army. He lost no time in marching forth to meet his unexpected assailants. The conflict was fierce but not prolonged. The French were soon defeated and put to flight. Quebec surrendered. But Montcalm did not make that surrender, nor did Wolfe receive it. Both generals fell in the battle. Wolfe died happy that the victory was gained. Montcalm was thankful that death spared him the humiliation of giving up Quebec. They died as enemies. But the men of a new generation, thinking less of the accidents which made them foes than of the noble courage and devotedness which united them, placed their names together upon the monument which marks out to posterity the scene of this decisive battle.

1827
A.D.

France did not quietly accept her defeat. Next year she made an attempt to regain Quebec. It was all in vain. In due time the success of the English resulted in a treaty of peace, under which France ceded to England all her claims upon Canada. Spain at the same time relinquished Florida. England had now undisputed possession of the western continent, from the region of perpetual winter to the Gulf of Mexico.

IV.

AMERICA ON THE EVE OF THE REVOLUTION.

A CENTURY and a half had now passed since the first colony had been planted on American soil. The colonists were fast ripening into fitness for independence. They had increased with marvellous rapidity. Europe never ceased to send forth her superfluous and needy thousands. America opened wide her hospitable arms and gave assurance of liberty and comfort to all who came. The thirteen colonies now contained a population of about three millions.

They were eminently a trading people, and their foreign commerce was already large and lucrative. New England built ships with the timber of her boundless forests, and sold them to foreign countries. She caught fish and sent them to the West Indies. She killed whales and sent the oil to England. New York and Pennsylvania produced wheat, which Spain and Portugal were willing to buy. Virginia clung to the tobacco-plant, which Europe was not then, any more than she is now, wise enough to dispense with. The swampy regions of Carolina and Georgia produced rice sufficient to supply the European demand. As yet cotton does not take any rank in the list of exports. But the time is near. Even now Richard Arkwright is brooding over improvements in the art of spinning cotton. When these are perfected the growing of cotton will rise quickly to a supremacy over all the industrial pursuits.

England had not learned to recognize the equality of her

colonists with her own people. The colonies were understood to exist not for their own good so much as for the good of the mother country. Even the chimney-sweepers, as Lord Chatham asserted, might be heard in the streets of London talking boastfully of their subjects in America. Colonies were settlements "established in distant parts of the world for the benefit of trade." As such they were most consistently treated. The Americans could not import direct any article of foreign production. Everything must be landed in England and re-shipped thence, that the English merchant might have profit. One exemption only was allowed from the operation of this law—the products of Africa, the unhappy negroes, were conveyed direct to America, and every possible encouragement was given to that traffic. Notwithstanding the illiberal restrictions of the home government, the imports of America before the Revolution had risen almost to the value of three millions sterling.

New England had, very early, established her magnificent system of Common Schools. For two or three generations these had been in full operation. The people of New England were now probably the most carefully instructed people in the world. There could not be found a person born in New England unable to read and write. It had always been the practice of the Northern people to settle in townships or villages where education was easily carried to them. In the South it had not been so. There the Common Schools had taken no root. It was impossible among a population so scattered. The educational arrangements of the South have never been adequate to the necessities of the people.

In the early years of America, the foundations were laid of those differences in character and interest which have since produced results of such magnitude. The men who peopled the Eastern States had to contend with a somewhat severe climate and a comparatively sterile soil. These disadvantages imposed upon them habits of industry and frugality. Skilled labour alone could be of use in their circumstances. They were thus mercifully rescued from the curse of slavery—by the absence of temptation, it may be, rather than by superiority of virtue. Their simple purity of manners remained long uncorrupted. The firm texture of mind which upheld them in their early difficulties remained unenfeebled. Their love of liberty was not perverted into a passion for supremacy. Among them labour was not degraded by becoming the function of a despised race. In New England labour has always been honourable. A just-minded, self-relying, self-helping people, vigorous in acting, patient in enduring—it was evident from the outset that they, at least, would not disgrace their ancestry.

The men of the South were very differently circumstanced. Their climate was delicious; their soil was marvellously fertile; their products were welcome in the markets of the world; unskilled labour was applicable in the rearing of all their great staples. Slavery being exceedingly profitable, struck deep roots very early. It was easy to grow rich. The colonists found themselves not the employers merely, but the owners of their labourers. They became aristocratic in feeling and in manners, resembling the picturesque chiefs of old Europe rather than mere prosaic growers of tobacco and rice. They had the virtues of chivalry, and also its vices. They were generous, open-handed, hospitable. But they were haughty and passionate, improvident, devoted to pleasure and amusement more than to work of any description. Living apart, each on his own plantation, the education of children was frequently imperfect, and the planter himself was bereft of that wholesome discipline to mind and to temper which residence among equals confers. The two great divisions of States—those in which slavery was profitable, and those in which it was unprofitable—were unequally yoked together. Their divergence of character and interest continued to increase, till it issued in one of the greatest of recorded wars.

Up to the year 1764, the Americans cherished a deep reverence and affection for the mother country. They were proud of her great place among the nations. They gloried in the splendour of her military achievements. They copied her manners and her fashions. She was in all things their model. They always spoke of England as "home." To be an Old England man was to be a person of rank and importance among them. They yielded a loving obedience to her laws. They were governed, as Benjamin Franklin stated it, at the expense of a little pen and ink. When money was asked from their Assemblies, it was given without grudge. "They were led by a thread,"—such was their love for the land which gave them birth.

Ten or twelve years came and went. A marvellous change has passed upon the temper of the American people. They have bound themselves by great oaths to use no article of English manufacture—to engage in no transaction which can put a shilling into any English pocket. They have formed "the inconvenient habit of carting"— that is, of tarring and feathering and dragging through the streets such persons as avow friendship for the English Government. They burn the Acts of the English Parliament by the hands of the common hangman. They slay the King's soldiers. They refuse every amicable proposal. They cast from them for ever the King's authority. They hand down a dislike to the English name, of which some traces lingered among them for generations.

By what unhallowed magic has this change been wrought so swiftly? By what process, in so few years, have three millions of people been taught to abhor the country they so loved?

The ignorance and folly of the English Government wrought this evil. But there is little cause for regret. Under the fuller knowledge of our modern time, colonies are allowed to discontinue their connection with the mother country when it is their wish to do so. Better had America gone in peace. But better she went, even in wrath and bloodshed, than continued in paralyzing dependence upon England.

For many years England had governed her American colonies harshly, and in a spirit of undisguised selfishness. America was ruled, not for her own good, but for the good of English commerce. She was not allowed to export her products except to England. No foreign ship might enter her ports. Woollen goods were not allowed to be sent from one colony to another. At one time the manufacture of hats was forbidden. In a liberal mood Parliament removed that prohibition, but decreed that no maker of hats should employ any negro workman, or any larger number of apprentices than two. Iron-works were forbidden. Up to the latest hour of English rule the Bible was not allowed to be printed in America.

The Americans had long borne the cost of their own government and defence. But in that age of small revenue and profuse expenditure on unmeaning continental wars, it had been often suggested that America should be taxed for the purposes of the home Government. Some one proposed that to Sir Robert Walpole in a time of need. The wise Sir Robert shook his head. It must be a bolder man than he was who would attempt that. A man bolder, because less wise, was found in due time.

1764
A.D.
The Seven Years' War had ended, and England had added a hundred millions to her national debt. The country was suffering, as countries always do after great wars, and it was no easy matter to fit the new burdens on to the national shoulder. The hungry eye of Lord Grenville searched where a new tax might be laid. The Americans had begun visibly to prosper. Already their growing wealth was the theme of envious discourse among English merchants. The

English officers who had fought in America spoke in glowing terms of the magnificent hospitality which had been extended to them. No more need be said. The House of Commons passed a resolution asserting their right to tax the Americans. No solitary voice was raised against this fatal resolution. Immediately after, an Act was passed imposing certain taxes upon silks, coffee, sugar, and other articles. The Americans remonstrated. They were willing, they said, to vote what moneys the King required of them, but they vehemently denied the right of any Assembly in which they were not represented to take from them any portion of their property. They were the subjects of the King, but they owed no obedience to the English Parliament. Lord Grenville went on his course. He had been told the Americans would complain but submit, and he believed it. Next session an Act was passed imposing Stamp Duties on America. The measure awakened no interest. Edmund Burke said he had never been present at a more languid debate. In the House of Lords there was no debate at all. With so little trouble was a continent rent away from the British Empire.

Benjamin Franklin told the House of Commons that America would never submit to the Stamp Act, and that no power on earth could enforce it. The Americans made it impossible for Government to mistake their sentiments. Riots, which swelled from day to day into dimensions more " enormous and alarming," burst forth in the New England States. Everywhere the stamp distributers were compelled to resign their offices. One unfortunate man was led forth to Boston Common, and made to sign his resignation in presence of a vast crowd. Another, in desperate health, was visited in his sick-room and obliged to pledge that if he lived he would resign. A universal resolution was come to that no English goods would be imported till the Stamp Act was repealed. The colonists would " eat nothing, drink nothing, wear

1765
A.D.

nothing, that comes from England," while this great injustice endured. The Act was to come into force on the 1st of November. That day the bells rang out funereal peals, and the colonists wore the aspect of men on whom some heavy calamity has fallen. But the Act never came into force. Not one of Lord Grenville's stamps was ever bought or sold in America. Some of the stamped paper was burned by the mob. The rest was hidden away to save it from the same fate. Without stamps, marriages were null; mercantile transactions ceased to be binding; suits at law were impossible. Nevertheless the business of human life went on. Men married; they bought, they sold; they went to law—illegally, because without stamps. But no harm came of it.

England heard with amazement that America refused to obey the law. There were some who demanded that the Stamp Act should be enforced by the sword. But it greatly moved the English merchants that America should cease to import their goods. William Pitt—not yet Earl of Chatham—denounced the Act, and said he was glad America had resisted. Pitt and the merchants triumphed, and the Act was repealed. There was illumination in the city that night. The city bells rang for joy. The ships in the Thames displayed all their colours. The saddest heart in all London was that of poor King George, who never ceased to lament "the fatal repeal of the Stamp Act." All America thrilled with joy and pride when news arrived of the great triumph. They voted Pitt a statue. They set apart a day for public rejoicing. All prisoners for debt were set free. A great deliverance had been granted, and the delight of the gladdened people knew no bounds. The danger is over for the present. But whosoever governs America now has need to walk warily.

1766
A.D.

It was during the agitation arising out of the Stamp Act that the idea of a General Congress of the States was suggested. A loud cry for union had arisen. "Join or die" was the prevailing sentiment. The Congress met in New York. It did little more than discuss and petition. It is interesting merely as one of the first exhibitions of a tendency towards federal union in a country whose destiny, in all coming time, this tendency was to fix.

The repeal of the Stamp Act delayed only for a little the fast-coming crisis. A new Ministry was formed, with the Earl of Chatham at its head. But soon the great Earl lay sick and helpless, and the burden of government rested on incapable shoulders. Charles Townshend, a clever, captivating, but most indiscreet man, became the virtual Prime Minister. The feeling in the public mind had now become more unfavourable to America. Townshend proposed to levy a variety of taxes from the Americans. The most famous of his taxes was one of three-pence per pound on tea. All his proposals became law.

This time the more thoughtful Americans began to despair of justice. The boldest scarcely ventured yet to suggest revolt against England, so powerful and so loved. But the grand final refuge of independence was silently brooded over by many. The mob fell back on their customary solution. Great riots occurred. To quell these disorders English troops encamped on Boston Common. The town swarmed with red-coated men, every one of whom was a humiliation. Their drums beat on Sabbath, and troubled the orderly men of Boston even in church. At intervals fresh transports dropped in, bearing additional soldiers, till a great force occupied the town. The galled citizens could ill brook to be thus bridled. The ministers prayed to Heaven for deliverance from the presence of the soldiers. The General Court of Massachusetts called vehemently on the Governor to remove them. The Governor had no powers in that matter. He called upon the court to make suitable provision for the King's troops, —a request which it gave the court infinite pleasure to refuse.

The universal irritation broke forth in frequent brawls between soldiers and people. One wintry moonlight night in March, when snow and ice lay about the streets of Boston, a more than usually determined attack was made upon a party of soldiers. The mob thought the soldiers dared not fire without the order of a magistrate, and were very bold in the strength of that belief. It proved a mistake. The soldiers did fire, and the blood of eleven slain or wounded persons stained the frozen streets. This was "the Boston Massacre," which greatly inflamed the patriot antipathy to the mother country.

1770 A.D.

Two or three unquiet years passed. No progress towards a settlement of differences had been made. From all the colonies there came, loud and unceasing, the voice of complaint and remonstrance. It fell upon unheeding ears. England was committed. To her honour be it said, it was not in the end for money that she alienated her children. The tax on tea must be maintained to vindicate the authority of England. But when the tea was shipped, such a drawback was allowed that the price would actually have been lower in America than it was at home.

The Americans had, upon the whole, kept loyally to their purpose of importing no English goods, specially no goods on which duty could be levied. Occasionally, a patriot of the more worldly-minded sort yielded to temptation, and secretly despatched an order to England. He was forgiven, if penitent. If obdurate, his name was published, and a resolution of the citizens to trade no more with a person so unworthy soon brought him to reason. But, in the main, the colonists were true to their bond, and when they could no longer smuggle they ceased to import. The East India Company accumulated vast quantities of unsaleable tea. A market must be found. Several ships were freighted with tea, and sent out to America. Cheaper tea was never seen in America, but it bore upon it the abhorred tax which asserted British control

1773 A.D.

over the property of Americans. Will the Americans, long bereaved of the accustomed beverage, yield to the temptation, and barter their honour for cheap tea? The East India Company never doubted it. But the Company knew nothing of the temper of the American people. The ships arrived at New York and Philadelphia. These cities stood firm. The ships were promptly sent home—their hatches unopened—and duly bore their rejected cargoes back to the Thames.

When the ships destined for Boston showed their tall masts in the bay, the citizens ran together to hold council. It was Sabbath, and the men of Boston were strict. But here was an exigency, in presence of which all ordinary rules are suspended. The crisis has come at length. If that tea is landed it will be sold, it will be used, and American liberty will become a byword upon the earth.

Samuel Adams was the true King in Boston at that time. He was a man in middle life, of cultivated mind and stainless reputation—a powerful speaker and writer—a man in whose sagacity and moderation all men trusted. He resembled the old Puritans in his stern love of liberty—his reverence for the Sabbath—his sincere, if somewhat formal, observance of all religious ordinances. He was among the first to see that there was no resting-place in this struggle short of independence. "We are free," he said, "and want no King." The men of Boston felt the power of his resolute spirit, and manfully followed where Samuel Adams led.

It was hoped that the agents of the East India Company would have consented to send the ships home. But the agents refused. Several days of excitement and ineffectual negotiation ensued. People flocked in from the neighbouring towns. The time was spent mainly in public meeting. The city resounded with impassioned discourse. But meanwhile the ships lay peacefully at their moorings, and the tide of patriot talk seemed to flow in vain. Other measures were visibly necessary. One day a meeting was held, and the excited people continued in hot debate till the shades of evening fell. No progress was made. At length Samuel Adams stood up in the dimly-lighted church, and announced, "This meeting can do nothing more to save the country." With a stern shout the meeting broke up. Fifty men disguised as Indians hurried down to the wharf, each man with a hatchet in his hand. The crowd followed. The ships were boarded; the chests of tea were brought on deck, broken up, and flung into the bay. The approving citizens looked on in silence. It was felt by all that the step was grave and eventful in the highest degree. So still was the crowd that no sound was heard but the stroke of the hatchet and the splash of the shattered chests as they fell into the sea. All questions about the disposal of those cargoes of tea at all events are now solved.

This is what America has done. It is for England to make the next move. Lord North was now at the head of the British Government. It was his lordship's belief that the troubles in America sprang from a small number of ambitious persons, and could easily, by proper firmness, be suppressed. "The Americans will be lions while we are lambs," said General Gage. The King believed this. Lord North believed it. In this deep ignorance he proceeded to deal with the great emergency. He closed Boston as a port for the landing and shipping of goods. He imposed a fine to indemnify the East India Company for their lost teas. He withdrew the Charter of Massachusetts. He authorized the Governor to send political offenders to England for trial. Great voices were raised against these severities. Lord Chatham, old in constitution now, if not in years, and near the close of his career, pled for measures of conciliation. Edmund Burke justified the resistance of the Americans. Their opposition was fruitless. All Lord North's measures of repression became law; and General Gage, with an additional force of soldiers, was sent to Boston to carry them into effect. Gage was an authority on American affairs. He had fought under Braddock. Among blind men the one-eyed man is king. Among the profoundly ignorant, the man with a little knowledge is irresistibly persuasive. "Four regiments sent to Boston," said the hopeful Gage, "will prevent any disturbance." He was believed; but, unhappily for his own comfort, he was sent to Boston to secure the fulfilment of his own prophecy. He threw up some fortifications and lay as in a hostile city. The Americans appointed a day of fasting and humiliation. They did more. They formed themselves into military companies. They occupied themselves with drill. They laid up stores of ammunition. Most of them had muskets, and could use them. He who had no musket now got one. They hoped that civil war would be averted, but there was no harm in being ready.

While General Gage was throwing up his fortifications at Boston, there met at Philadelphia a Congress of delegates, sent by the States, to confer in regard to the troubles which were thickening round them. Twelve States were represented. Georgia as yet paused timidly on the brink of the perilous enterprise. They were notable men who met there, and their work is held in enduring honour. "For genuine sagacity, for singular moderation, for solid wisdom," said the great Earl of Chatham, "the Congress of Philadelphia shines unrivalled." The low-roofed quaint old room in which their meetings were held, became one of the shrines which Americans delight to visit. George Washington was there, and his massive sense and copious knowledge were a supreme guiding power. Patrick Henry, then a young man, brought to the council a wisdom beyond his years, and a fiery eloquence, which, to some of his hearers, seemed almost more

Sept. 5,
1774
A.D.

than human. He had already proved his unfitness for farming and for shop-keeping. He was now to prove that he could utter words which swept over a continent, thrilling men's hearts like the voice of the trumpet, and rousing them to heroic deeds. John Routledge from South Carolina aided him with an eloquence little inferior to his own. Richard Henry Lee, with his Roman aspect, his bewitching voice, his ripe scholarship, his rich stores of historical and political knowledge, would have graced the highest assemblies of the Old World. John Dickenson, the wise farmer from the banks of the Delaware, whose Letters had done so much to form the public sentiment—his enthusiastic love of England overborne by his sense of wrong— took regretful but resolute part in withstanding the tyranny of the English Government.

We have the assurance of Washington that the members of this Congress did not aim at independence. As yet it was their wish to have wrongs redressed and to continue British subjects. Their proceedings give ample evidence of this desire. They drew up a narrative of their wrongs. As a means of obtaining redress, they adopted a resolution that all commercial intercourse with Britain should cease. They addressed the King, imploring his majesty to remove those grievances which endangered their relations with him. They addressed the people of Great Britain, with whom, they said, they deemed a union as their greatest glory and happiness; adding, however, that they would not be hewers of wood and drawers of water to any nation in the world. They appealed to their brother colonists of Canada for support in their peaceful resistance to oppression. But Canada, newly conquered from France, was peopled almost wholly by Frenchmen. A Frenchman of that time was contented to enjoy such an amount of liberty and property as his King was pleased to permit. And so from Canada there came no response of sympathy or help.

Here Congress paused. Some members believed, with Washington, that their remonstrances would be effectual. Others, less sanguine, looked for no settlement but that which the sword might bring. They adjourned, to meet again next May. This is enough for the present. What further steps the new events of that coming summer may call for, we shall be prepared, with God's help, to take.

England showed no relenting in her treatment of the Americans. The King gave no reply to the address of Congress. The Houses of Lords and of Commons refused even to allow that address to be read in their hearing. The King announced his firm purpose to reduce the refractory colonists to obedience. Parliament gave loyal assurances of support to the blinded monarch. All trade with the colonies was forbidden. All American ships and cargoes might be seized by those who were strong enough to do so. The alternative presented to the American choice was without disguise. The Americans had to fight for their liberty, or forego it. The people of England had, in those days, no control over the government of their country. All this was managed for them by a few great families. Their allotted part was to toil hard, pay their taxes, and be silent. If they had been permitted to speak, their voice would have vindicated the men who asserted the right of self-government—a right which Englishmen themselves were not to enjoy for many a long year.

General Gage had learned that considerable stores of ammunition were collected at the village of Concord, eighteen miles from Boston. He would seize them in the King's name. Late one April night eight hundred soldiers set out on this errand. They hoped their coming would be unexpected, as care had been taken to prevent the tidings from being carried out of Boston. But as they marched, the

1775
A.D.

clang of bells and the firing of guns gave warning far and near of their approach. In the early morning they reached Lexington. Some hours before, a body of militia awaited them there. But the morning was chill and the hour untimely. The patriots were allowed to seek the genial shelter of the tavern. They were pledged to appear at beat of drum. Seventy of them did so, mostly, we are told, "in a confused state." Major Pitcairn commanded them to disperse. The patriots did not at once obey the summons. It was impossible that seventy volunteers could mean to fight eight hundred British soldiers. It is more likely they did not clearly understand what was required of them. Firing ensued. The Americans say that the first shot came from the British. Major Pitcairn always asserted that he himself saw a countryman give the first fire from behind a wall. It can never be certainly known. There was now firing enough. The British stood and shot, in their steady unconcerned way, at the poor mistaken seventy. The patriots fled fast. Eighteen of their number did not join the flight. These lay in their blood on the village green, dead or wounded men. Thus was the war begun between England and her colonies.

The British pushed on to Concord, and destroyed all the military stores they could find. It was not much, for there had been time to carry off nearly everything. By noon the work was done, and the wearied troops turned their faces towards Boston.

They were not suffered to march alone. All that morning grim-faced yeomen—of the Ironside type, each man with a musket in his hand—had been hurrying into Concord. The British march was mainly on a road cut through dense woods. As they advanced, the vengeful yeomanry hung upon their flanks and rear. On every side there streamed forth an incessant and murderous fire. The men fell fast. No effort could dislodge those deadly but almost unseen foes. During all the terrible hours of that return march the fire of the Americans never flagged, and could seldom be returned. It was sunset ere the soldiers, half dead with fatigue, got home to Boston. In killed, wounded, and prisoners, this fatal expedition had cost nearly three hundred men. The blood shed at Lexington had been swiftly and deeply avenged.

V.

BUNKER HILL.

The encounters at Lexington and Concord thoroughly aroused the American people. The news rang through the land that blood had been spilt—that already there were martyrs to the great cause. Mounted couriers galloped along all highways. Over the bustle of the market-place—in the stillness of the quiet village church—there broke the startling shout, "The war has begun." All men felt that the hour had come, and they promptly laid aside their accustomed labour that they might gird themselves for the battle. North Carolina, in her haste, threw off the authority of the King, and formed herself into military companies. Timid Georgia sent gifts of money and of rice, and cheering letters, to confirm the bold purposes of the men of Boston. In aristocratic and loyal Virginia there was a general rush to arms. From every corner of the New England States men hurried to Boston. Down in pleasant Connecticut an old man was ploughing his field one April afternoon. His name was Israel Putnam. He was now a farmer and tavern-keeper—a combination frequent at that time in New England, and not at all inconsistent, we are told, "with a Roman character." Formerly he had been a warrior. He had fought the Indians, and had narrowly escaped the jeopardies of such warfare. Once he had been bound to a tree, and the savages were beginning to toss their tomahawks at his head, when unhoped-for rescue found him. As rugged old Israel ploughed his field, some one told him of Lexington. That day he ploughed no more. He sent word home that he had gone to Boston. Unyoking his horse from the plough, in a few minutes he was mounted and hastening towards the camp.

Boston and its suburbs stand on certain islets and peninsulas, access to which, from the mainland, is gained by one isthmus which is called Boston Neck, and another isthmus which is called Charlestown Neck. A city thus circumstanced is not difficult to blockade. The American Yeomanry blockaded Boston. There were five thousand soldiers in the town; but the retreat from Concord inclined General Gage to some measure of patient endurance, and he made no attempt to raise the blockade.

The month of May was wearing on. Still General Gage lay inactive. Still patriot Americans poured in to the blockading camp. They were utterly undisciplined. They were without uniform. The English scorned them as a rabble "with calico frocks and fowling-pieces." But they were Anglo-Saxons with arms in their hands, and a fixed purpose in their minds. It was very likely that the unwise contempt of their enemies would not be long unrebuked.

On the 25th, several English ships of war dropped their anchors in Boston Bay. It was rumoured that they brought large reinforcements under Howe, Burgoyne, and Clinton—the best generals England possessed. Shortly it became known that Gage now felt himself strong enough to break out upon his rustic besiegers. But the choice of time and place for the encounter was not to be left with General Gage.

On Charlestown peninsula, within easy gun-shot of Boston, there are two low hills, one of which, the higher, is called Bunker Hill, and the other Breed's Hill. In a council of war the Americans determined to seize and fortify one of these heights, and there abide the onslaught of the English. There was not a moment to lose. It was said that Gage intended to occupy the heights on the night of the 18th June. But Gage was habitually too late. On the 16th, a little before sunset, twelve hundred Americans were mustered on Cambridge Common for special service. Colonel Prescott, a veteran who had fought against the French, was in command. Putnam was with him, to be useful where he could, although without specified duties. Prayers were said; and the men, knowing only that they went to battle, and perhaps to death, set forth upon their march. They marched in silence, for their way led them under the guns of English ships. They reached the hill-top undiscovered by the supine foe. It was a lovely June night—warm and still. Far down lay the English ships—awful, but as yet harmless. Across the Charles river, Boston and her garrison slept the sleep of the unsuspecting. The "All's well" of the sentinel crept, from time to time, dreamily up the hill. Swift now with spade and mattock, for the hours of this midsummer night are few and precious—swift, but cautious, too, for one ringing stroke of iron upon stone may ruin all!

When General Gage looked out upon the heights next morning, he saw a strong intrenchment and swarms of armed men where the untrodden grass had waved in the summer breeze a few hours before. He looked long through his glass at this unwelcome apparition. A tall figure paced to and fro along the rude parapet. It was Prescott. "Will he fight?" asked Gage eagerly. "Yes, sir," replied a bystander; "to the last drop of his blood."

It was indispensable that the works should be taken. A plan of attack was immediately formed. It was sufficiently simple. No one supposed that the Americans would stand the shock of regular troops. The English were therefore to march straight up the hill and drive the Americans away. Meanwhile reinforcements were sent to the Americans, and supplies of ammunition were distributed. A gill of powder, to be carried in a powder-horn or loose in the pocket, two flints and fifteen balls, were served out to each man. To obtain even the fifteen balls, they had to melt down the organ-pipes of an Episcopal church at Cambridge.

At noon English soldiers to the number of two thousand crossed over from Boston. The men on the hill-top looked out from their intrenchments upon a splendid vision of bright uniforms and bayonets and field-pieces flashing in the sun. They looked with quickened pulse but unshaken purpose. To men of their race it is not given to know fear on the verge of battle.

The English soldiers paused for refreshments when they landed on the Charlestown peninsula. The Americans could hear the murmur of their noisy talk and laughter. They saw the pitchers of grog pass along the ranks. And then they saw the Englishmen rise and stretch themselves to their grim morning's work. From the steeples and house-tops of Boston—from all the heights which stand round about the city—thousands of Americans watched the progress of the fight.

The soldiers had no easy task before them. The day was "exceeding hot," the grass was long and thick, the up-hill march was toilsome, the enemy watchful and resolute. As if to render the difficulty greater, the men carried three days' provision with them in their knapsacks. Each man had a burden which weighed one hundred and twenty pounds in knapsack, musket, and other equipments. Thus laden they began their perilous ascent.

While yet a long way from the enemy they opened a harmless fire of musketry. There was no reply from the American lines. Putnam had directed the men to withhold their fire till they could see the whites of the Englishmen's eyes, and then to aim low. The Englishmen were very near the works when the word was given. Like the left-handed slingers of the tribe of

Benjamin, the Americans could shoot to a hairbreadth. Every man took his steady aim, and when they gave forth their volley few bullets sped in vain. The slaughter was enormous. The English recoiled in some confusion, a pitiless rain of bullets following them down the hill. Again they advanced almost to the American works, and again they sustained a bloody repulse. And now, at the hill-foot, they laid down their knapsacks and stripped off their great-coats. They were resolute this time to end the fight by the bayonet. The American ammunition was exhausted. They could give the enemy only a single volley. The English swarmed over the parapet. The Americans had no bayonets, but for a time they waged unequal war with stones and the but-ends of their muskets. They were soon driven out, and fled down the hill and across the Neck to Cambridge, the English ships raking them with grape-shot as they ran.

They had done their work. Victory no doubt remained with the English. Their object was to carry the American intrenchments, and they had carried them. Far greater than this was the gain of the Americans. It was proved that, with the help of some slight field-works, it was possible for undisciplined patriots to meet on equal terms the best troops England could send against them. Henceforth the success of the Revolution was assured. "Thank God," said Washington, when he heard of the battle, "the liberties of the country are safe." Would that obstinate King George could have been made to see it! But many wives must be widows, and many children fatherless, before those dull eyes will open to the unwelcome truth.

Sixteen hundred men lay, dead or wounded, on that fatal slope. The English had lost nearly eleven hundred; the Americans nearly five hundred. Seldom indeed in any battle has so large a proportion of the combatants fallen.

The Americans, who had thus taken up arms and resisted

and slain the King's troops, were wholly without authority for what they had done. No governing body of any description had employed them or recognized them. What were still more alarming deficiencies, they were without a general, and without adequate supply of food and ammunition. Congress now, by a unanimous vote, adopted the army, and elected George Washington Commander-in-Chief of the patriot forces. They took measures to enlist soldiers, and to raise money for their support.

1775 A.D.

When Washington reached the army before Boston, he found it to consist of 14,000 men. They were quite undisciplined. They were almost without ammunition. Their stock of powder would afford only nine rounds to each man. They could thus have made no use of their artillery. Their rude intrenchments stretched a distance of eight or nine miles. At any moment the English might burst upon them, piercing their weak lines, and rolling them back in hopeless rout. But the stubborn provincials were, as yet, scarcely soldiers enough to know their danger. Taking counsel only of their own courage, they strengthened their intrenchment, and tenaciously maintained their hold on Boston.

From a convenient hill-top Washington looked at his foe. He saw a British army of 10,000 men, perfect in discipline and equipment. It was a noble engine, but, happily for the world, it was guided by incompetent hands. General Gage tamely endured siege without daring to strike a single blow at the audacious patriots. It was no easy winter in either army. The English suffered from small-pox. Their fleet failed to secure for them an adequate supply of food. They had to pull down houses to obtain wood for fuel, at the risk of being hanged if they were discovered. They were dispirited by long inaction. They knew that in England the feeling entertained about them was one of bitter disappointment. Poor Gage was recalled by an angry Ministry, and quitted in disgrace that Boston where he had hoped for such success. General Howe succeeded to his command, and to his policy of inactivity.

Washington on his side was often in despair. His troops were mainly enlisted for three months only. Their love of country gave way under the hardships of a soldier's life. Washington was a strict disciplinarian, and many a free-born back was scored by the lash. Patriotism proved a harder service than the men counted for. Fast as their time of service expired they set their faces homeward. Washington plied them with patriotic appeals, and even caused patriot songs to be sung about the camp. Not thus, however, could the self-indulgent men of Massachusetts and Connecticut be taught to scorn delights and live laborious days. "Such dearth of public spirit," Washington writes, "and such want of virtue, such fertility in all the low arts, I never saw before." When January **1776** A.D. came he had a new army, much smaller than the old, and the same weary process of drilling began afresh.

He knew that Howe was aware of his position. The inactivity of the English general astonished Washington. He could explain it no otherwise than by believing that Providence watched over the liberties of the American people.

In February liberal supplies of arms and ammunition reached him. There came also ten regiments of militia. Washington was now strong enough to take a step.

To the south of Boston city lie the Heights of Dorchester. If the Americans can seize and hold these heights, the English must quit Boston. The night of the 4th of March was fixed for the enterprise. A heavy fire of artillery occupied the attention of the enemy. By the light of an unclouded moon a strong working-party took their way to Dorchester Heights. A long train of waggons accompanied them, laden with hard-pressed bales of hay. These were needed to form a breastwork, as a hard frost bound the earth, and digging alone could not be relied upon. The men worked with such spirit, that by dawn the bales of hay had been fashioned into various redoubts and other defences of most formidable aspect. A thick fog lay along the heights, and the new fortress looked massive and imposing in the haze. "The rebels," said Howe, "have done more work in one night than my whole army would have done in a month."

And now the English must fight, or yield up Boston. The English chose to fight. They were in the act of embarking to get at the enemy when a furious east wind began to blow, scattering their transports and compelling the delay of the attack. All next day the storm continued to rage. The English, eager for battle, lay in unwilling idleness. The vigorous Americans never ceased to dig and build. On the third day the storm abated. But it was now General Howe's opinion that the American position was impregnable. It may be that he was wisely cautious. It may be that he was merely fearful. But he laid aside his thoughts of battle, and prepared to evacuate Boston. On the 17th the last English soldier was on board, and all New England was finally wrested from King George.

VI.

INDEPENDENCE.

Even yet, after months of fighting, the idea of final separation from Great Britain was distasteful to a large portion of the American people. To the more enlightened it had long been evident that no other course was possible. But very many still clung to the hope of a friendly settlement of differences. Some, who were native Englishmen, loved the land of their birth better than the land of their adoption. The Quakers and Moravians were opposed to war as sinful, and would content themselves with such redress as could be obtained by remonstrance. Some, who deeply resented the oppressions of the home Government, were slow to relinquish the privilege of British citizenship. Some would willingly have fought had there been hope of success, but could not be convinced that America was able to defend herself against the colossal strength of England. The subject was discussed long and keenly. The intelligence of America was in favour of separation. All the writers of the colonies urged incessantly that to this it must come. Endless pamphlets and gazette articles set forth the oppressions of the old country, and the need of independence in order to the welfare of the colonies. Conspicuous among those whose writings aided in convincing the public mind stands the unhonoured name of Thomas Paine the infidel. Paine had been only a few months in the colonies, but his restless mind took a ready interest in the great question of the day. He had a surprising power of direct, forcible argument. He wrote a pamphlet styled "Common Sense," in which he urged the Americans to be independent. His treatise had, for those days, a vast circulation, and an extraordinary influence.

The time was now ripe for the consideration by Congress of the great question of Independence. It was a grave and most eventful step, which no thinking man would lightly take, but it could no longer be shunned. On the 7th of June a resolution was introduced, declaring "That the United Colonies are and ought to be free and independent." The House was not yet prepared for a measure so decisive. Many members still paused on the threshold of that vast change. Pennsylvania and Delaware had expressly enjoined their delegates to oppose it; for the Quakers were loyal to the last. Some other States had given no instructions, and their delegates felt themselves bound, in consequence, to vote against the change. Seven States voted for the resolution; six voted against it. Greater unanimity than this was indispensable. With much prudence it was agreed that the matter should stand over for two or three weeks.

1776
A.D.

On the 4th of July the Declaration of Independence was adopted, with the unanimous concurrence of all the States. In this famous document the usurpations of the English Government were set forth in unsparing terms. The divinity which doth hedge a King did not protect poor King George from a rougher handling than he ever experienced before. His character, it was said, "was marked by every act which can define a tyrant." And then it was announced to the world that the Thirteen Colonies had terminated their political connection with Great Britain, and entered upon their career as free and independent States.

The vigorous action of Congress nerved the colonists for their great enterprise. The paralyzing hope of reconciliation was extinguished. The quarrel must now be fought out to the end, and liberty must be gloriously won or shamefully lost. Everywhere the Declaration was hailed with joy. It was read to the army amidst exulting shouts. The soldiers in New York expressed their transference of allegiance by taking down a leaden statue of King George and casting it into bullets to be used against the King's troops. Next day Washington, in the dignified language which was habitual to him, reminded his troops of their new duties and responsibilities. "The General," he said, "hopes and trusts that every officer and soldier will endeavour so to live and act as becomes a Christian soldier, defending the dearest rights and liberties of his country."

VII.

AT WAR.

ENGLAND put forth as much strength as she deemed needful to subdue her rebellious colonists. She prepared a strong fleet and a strong army. She entered into contracts with some of the petty German princes to supply a certain number of soldiers. It was a matter of regular sale and purchase. England supplied money at a fixed rate. The Duke of Brunswick and some others supplied a stipulated number of men, who were to shed their blood in a quarrel of which they knew nothing. Even in a dark age these transactions were a scandal. Frederick of Prussia loudly expressed his contempt for both parties. When any of the hired men passed through any part of his territory he levied on them the toll usually charged for cattle—like which, he said, they had been sold!

So soon as the safety of Boston was secured, Washington moved with his army southwards to New York. Thither, in the month of June, came General Howe. Thither also came his brother, Lord Howe, with the forces which England had provided for this war. These reinforcements raised the British army to 25,000 men. Lord Howe brought with him a commission from King George to pacify the dissatisfied colonists. He invited them to lay down their arms, and he assured them of the King's pardon. His proposals were singularly inopportune. The Declaration of Independence had just been published.

The Americans had determined to be free. They were not seeking to be forgiven, and they rejected with scorn Lord Howe's proposals. The sword must now decide between King George and his alienated subjects.

Lord Howe encamped his troops on Staten Island, a few miles from New York. His powerful fleet gave him undisputed command of the bay, and enabled him to choose his point of attack. The Americans expected that he would land upon Long Island, and take possession of the heights near Brooklyn. He would then be separated from New York only by a narrow arm of the sea, and he could with ease lay the city in ruins. Washington sent a strong force to hold the heights, and throw up intrenchments in front of Brooklyn. General Putnam was appointed to the command of this army. Staten Island lies full in view of Brooklyn. The white tents of the English army, and the formidable English ships lying at their anchorage, were watched by many anxious eyes. For the situation was known to be full of peril. Washington himself did not expect success in the coming fight, and hoped for nothing more than that the enemy's victory would cost him dear.

After a time it was seen that a movement was in progress among the English. One by one the tents disappeared. One by one the ships shook their canvas out to the wind, and moved across the bay. Then the Americans knew that their hour of trial was at hand.

Putnam marched his men out from their lines to meet the English. At daybreak the enemy made his appearance. The right wing of the American army was attacked, and troops were withdrawn from other points to resist what seemed the main attack. Meanwhile a strong English force made its way unseen round the American left, and established itself between the Americans and their intrenchments. This decided the fate of the battle.

Aug. 27, **1776** A.D.

The Americans made a brave but vain defence. They were driven within their lines after sustaining heavy loss.

Lord Howe could easily have stormed the works, and taken or destroyed the American army. But his lordship felt that his enemy was in his power, and he wished to spare his soldiers the bloodshed which an assault would have caused. He was to reduce the enemy's works by regular siege. It was no part of Washington's intention to wait for the issue of these operations. During the night of the 29th he silently withdrew his broken troops, and landed them safely in New York. So skilfully was this movement executed, that the last boat had pushed off from the shore before the British discovered that their enemies had departed.

But now New York had to be abandoned. Washington's army was utterly demoralized by the defeat at Brooklyn. The men went home, in some instances, by entire regiments. Washington confessed to the President of Congress with deep concern that he had no confidence "in the generality of the troops." To fight the well-disciplined and victorious British with such men was worse than useless. He marched northwards, and took up a strong position at Haerlem, a village nine miles from New York. But the English ships, sweeping up the Hudson river, showed themselves on his flank and in his rear. The English army approached him in front. There was no choice but retreat. Washington crossed his soldiers over to the Jersey side of the river. The English followed him, after storming a fort in which nearly three thousand men had been left, the whole of whom were made prisoners.

The fortunes of the revolted colonies were now at the very lowest ebb. Washington had only 4000 men under his immediate command. They were in miserable condition—imperfectly armed, poorly fed and clothed, without blankets, or tents, or shoes. An English officer said of them, without extreme exaggeration, "In a whole regiment there is scarce one pair of breeches." This was the army which was to snatch a continent from the grasp of England! As they marched towards Philadelphia the people looked with derision upon their ragged defenders, and with fear upon the brilliant host of pursuers. Lord Howe renewed his offer of pardon to all who would submit. This time his lordship's offers commanded some attention. Many of the wealthier patriots took the oath, and made their peace with a Government whose authority there was no longer any hope of throwing off.

Washington made good his retreat to Philadelphia, so hotly pursued that his rear-guard, engaged in pulling down bridges, were often in sight of the British pioneers sent to build them up. When he crossed the Delaware he secured all the boats for a distance of seventy miles along the river-course. Lord Howe was brought to a pause, and he decided to wait upon the eastern bank till the river should be frozen.

Washington knew well the desperate odds against him. He expected to be driven from the Eastern States. It was his thought, in that case, to retire beyond the Alleghanies, and in the wilderness to maintain undying resistance to the English yoke. Meantime he strove like a brave strong man to win back success to the patriot cause. It was only now that he was able to rid himself of the evil of short enlistments. Congress resolved that henceforth men should be enlisted to serve out the war.

Winter came, but Lord Howe remained inactive. He himself was in New York; his army was scattered about among the villages of New Jersey—fearing no evil from the despised Americans. All the time Washington was increasing the number of his troops, and improving their condition. But something was needed to chase away the gloom which paralyzed the country. Ten miles from Philadelphia was the village of

Trenton, held by a considerable force of British and Hessians. At sunset on Christmas evening Washington marched out from Philadelphia, having prepared a surprise for the careless garrison of Trenton. The night was dark and tempestuous, and the weather was so intensely cold that two of the soldiers were frozen to death. The march of the barefooted host could be tracked by the blood-marks which they left upon the snow. At daybreak they burst upon the astonished Royalists. The Hessians had drunk deep on the previous day, and they were ill prepared to fight. Their commander was slain as he attempted to bring his men up to the enemy. After his fall the soldiers laid down their arms, and surrendered at discretion.

A week after this encounter three British regiments spent a night at Princeton, on their way to Trenton to retrieve the disaster which had there befallen their Hessian allies. Washington made another night march, attacked the Englishmen in the early morning, and after a stubborn resistance defeated them, inflicting severe loss.

1777 A.D.

These exploits, inconsiderable as they seem, raised incalculably the spirits of the American people. When triumphs like these were possible under circumstances so discouraging, there was no need to despair of the Commonwealth. Confidence in Washington had been somewhat shaken by the defeats which he had sustained. Henceforth it was unbounded. Congress invested him with absolute military authority for a period of six months, and public opinion confirmed the trust. The infant Republic was delivered from its most imminent jeopardy by the apparently trivial successes of Trenton and Princeton.

VIII.

SYMPATHY BEYOND THE SEA.

France still felt, with all the bitterness of the vanquished, her defeat at Quebec and her loss of Canada. She had always entertained the hope that the Americans would avenge her by throwing off the English yoke. To help forward its fulfilment, she sent occasionally a secret agent among them, to cultivate their good-will to the utmost. When the troubles began she sent secret assurances of sympathy, and secret offers of commercial advantages. She was not prepared as yet openly to espouse the American cause. But it was always safe to encourage the American dislike to England, and to connive at the fitting out of American privateers, to prey upon English commerce.

The Marquis de Lafayette was at this time serving in the French army. He was a lad of nineteen, of immense wealth, and enjoying a foremost place among the nobility of France. The American revolt had now become a topic at French dinner-tables. Lafayette heard of it first from the Duke of Gloucester, who told the story at a dinner given to him by some French officers. That conversation changed the destiny of the young Frenchman. "He was a man of no ability," said Napoleon. "There is nothing in his head but the United States," said Marie Antoinette. These judgments are perhaps not unduly severe. But Lafayette had the deepest sympathies with the cause of human liberty. They may not have been always wise, but they were always generous and true. No sooner had he satisfied himself that the American cause was the cause of liberty, than he hastened to ally himself with it. He left his young wife and his great position, and he offered himself to Washington. His military value may not have been great; but his presence was a vast encouragement to a desponding people. He was a visible assurance of sympathy beyond the sea. America is the most grateful of nations; and this good, impulsive, vain man has ever deservedly held a high place in her love. Washington once, with tears of joy in his eyes, presented Lafayette to his troops. Counties are named after him, and cities and streets. Statues and paintings hand down to successive generations of Americans the image of their first and most faithful ally.

Lafayette was the lightning-rod by which the current of republican sentiments was flashed from America to France. He came home when the war was over and America free. He was the hero of the hour. A man who had helped to set up a Republic in America was an unquiet element for old France to receive back into her bosom. With the charm of a great name and boundless popularity to aid him, he everywhere urged that men should be free and self-governing. Before he had been long in France he was busily stirring up the oppressed Protestants of the south to revolt. Happily the advice of Washington, with whom he continued to correspond, arrested a course which might have led the enthusiastic Marquis to the scaffold. Few men of capacity so moderate have been so conspicuous, or have so powerfully influenced the course of human affairs.

IX.

THE WAR CONTINUES.

1777
A.D.

SPRING-TIME came—"the time when Kings go out to battle" —but General Howe was not ready. Washington was contented to wait, for he gained by delay. Congress sent him word that he was to lose no time in totally subduing the enemy. Washington could now afford to smile at the vain confidence which had so quickly taken the place of despair. Recruits flowed in upon him in a steady, if not a very copious stream. The old soldiers whose terms expired were induced, by bounties and patriotic appeals, to re-enlist for the war. By the middle of June, when Howe opened the campaign, Washington had 8000 men under his command, tolerably armed and disciplined, and in good fighting spirit. The patriotic sentiment was powerfully reinforced by a thirst to avenge private wrongs. Howe's German mercenaries had behaved very brutally in New Jersey—plundering and burning without stint. Many of the Americans had witnessed outrages such as turn the coward's blood to flame.

Howe wished to take Philadelphia, then the political capital of the States. But Washington lay across his path, in a strong position, from which he could not be enticed to descend. Howe marched towards him, but shunned to attack him where he lay. Then he turned back to New York, and embarking his troops, sailed with them to Philadelphia. The army was landed on the

25th August, and Howe was at length ready to begin the summer's work.

The American army waited for him on the banks of a small river called the Brandywine. The British superiority in numbers enabled them to attack the Americans in front and in flank. The Americans say that their right wing, on which the British attack fell with crushing weight, was badly led. One of the generals of that division was a certain William Alexander—known to himself and the country of his adoption as Lord Stirling—a warrior brave but foolish; "aged, and a little deaf." The Americans were driven from the field, but they had fought bravely, and were undismayed by their defeat.

A fortnight later a British force, with Lord Cornwallis at its head, marched into Philadelphia. The Royalists were strong in that city of Quakers—specially strong among the Quakers themselves. The city was moved to unwonted cheerfulness. On that September morning, as the loyal inhabitants looked upon the bright uniforms and flashing arms of the King's troops, and listened to the long-forbidden strains of "God save the King," they felt as if a great and final deliverance had been vouchsafed to them. The patriots estimated the fall of the city more justly. It was seen that if Howe meant to hold Philadelphia, he had not force enough to do much else. Said the sagacious Benjamin Franklin,—"It is not General Howe that has taken Philadelphia; it is Philadelphia that has taken General Howe."

The main body of the British were encamped at Germantown, guarding their new conquest. So little were the Americans daunted by their late reverses, that, within a week from the capture of Philadelphia, Washington resolved to attack the enemy. At sunrise on the 4th October the English were unexpectedly greeted by a bayonet-charge from a strong American force. It was a complete surprise, and at first the success was complete. But a dense fog, which had rendered the surprise possible, ultimately frustrated the purpose of the assailants. The onset of the eager Americans carried all before it. But as the darkness, enhanced by the firing, deepened over the combatants, confusion began to arise. Regiments got astray from their officers. Some regiments mistook each other for enemies, and acted on that belief. Confusion swelled to panic, and the Americans fled from the field.

Winter was now at hand, and the British army returned to quarters in Philadelphia. Howe would have fought again, but Washington declined to come down from the strong position to which he had retired. His army had again been suffered to fall into straits which threatened its very existence. A patriot Congress urged him to defeat the English, but could not be persuaded to supply his soldiers with shoes or blankets, or even with food. He was advised to fall back on some convenient town where his soldiers would find the comforts they needed so much. But Washington was resolute to keep near the enemy. He fixed on a position at Valley Forge, among the hills, twenty miles from Philadelphia. Thither through the snow marched his half-naked army. Log-huts were erected with a rapidity of which no soldiers are so capable as Americans. There Washington fixed himself. The enemy was within reach, and he knew that his own strength would grow. The campaign which had now closed had given much encouragement to the patriots. It is true they had been often defeated. But they had learned to place implicit confidence in their commander. They had learned also that in courage they were equal, in activity greatly superior, to their enemies. All they required was discipline and experience, which another campaign would give. There was no longer any reason to look with alarm upon the future.

X.

THE SURRENDER AT SARATOGA.

In the month of June, when Howe was beginning to win his lingering way to Philadelphia, a British army set out from Canada to conquer the northern parts of the revolted territory. General Burgoyne was in command. He was resolute to succeed. "This army must not retreat," he said when they were about to embark. The army did not retreat. On a fair field general and soldiers would have played a part of which their country would have had no cause to be ashamed. But this was a work beyond their strength.

1777
A.D.

Burgoyne marched deep into the New England States. But he had to do with men of a different temper from those of New York and Philadelphia. At his approach every man took down his musket from the wall and hurried to the front. Little discipline had they, but a resolute purpose and a sure aim. Difficulties thickened around the fated army. At length Burgoyne found himself at Saratoga. It was now October. Heavy rains fell. Provisions were growing scanty. The enemy was in great force, and much emboldened by success. Gradually it became evident that the British were surrounded, and that no hope of fighting their way out remained. Night and day a circle of fire encompassed them. Burgoyne called his officers together. They could find no place for their sorrowful communing beyond reach of the enemy's musketry, so closely was the net already drawn. There was but one thing to do, and it was done. The British army surrendered. Nearly six thousand brave men, in sorrow and in shame, laid down their arms. The men who took them were mere peasants. No two of them were dressed alike. The officers wore uncouth wigs. Most of them carried muskets and large powder-horns slung around their shoulders. No humiliation like this had ever befallen the British arms.

These grotesque American warriors behaved to their conquered enemies with true nobility. General Gates, the American commander, kept his men strictly within their lines, that they might not witness the piling of the British arms. No taunt was offered, no look of disrespect was directed against the fallen. "All were mute in astonishment and pity."

England felt acutely the shame of this great disaster. Her people were used to victory. For many years she had been fighting in Europe, in India, in Canada, and always with brilliant success. Her defeat in America was contrary to all expectation. It was a bitter thing for a high-spirited people to hear that their veteran troops had surrendered to a crowd of half-armed peasantry. Under the depressing influence of this calamity it was determined to redress the wrongs of America. Parliament abandoned all claim to tax the colonies. Every vexatious enactment would be repealed. All would be forgiven, if America would return to her allegiance. Commissioners were sent bearing the olive-branch to Congress. Too late—altogether too late! Never more can America be a dependency of England. With few words Congress peremptorily declined the English overtures. America had chosen her course. For good or for evil she would follow it to the end.

XI.

HELP FROM EUROPE.

A GREAT war may be very glorious, but it is also very miserable. Twenty thousand Englishmen had already perished in this war. Trade languished, and among the working-classes there was want of employment and consequent want of food. American cruisers swarmed upon the sea, and inflicted enormous losses upon English commerce. The debt of the country increased. And for all these evils there was no compensation. There was not even the poor satisfaction of success in our unprofitable undertaking.

1778 A.D.

If it was any comfort to inflict even greater miseries than she endured, England did not fight in vain. The sufferings of America were very lamentable. The loss of life in battle and by disease, resulting from want and exposure, had been great. The fields in many districts were unsown. Trade was extinct; the trading classes were bankrupt. English cruisers had annihilated the fisheries and seized the greater part of the American merchant ships. Money had well-nigh disappeared from the country. Congress issued paper money, which proved a very indifferent substitute. The public had so little confidence in the new currency, that Washington declared, " A waggon-load of money will scarcely purchase a waggon-load of provisions."

But the war went on. It was not for England, with her high place among the nations, to retire defeated from an enterprise on which she had deliberately entered. As for the Americans, after they had declared their resolution to be independent, they could die, but they could not yield.

The surrender of Burgoyne brought an important ally to the American side. The gods help those who help themselves. So soon as America proved that she was likely to conquer in the struggle, France offered to come to her aid. France had always looked with interest on the war; partly because she hated England, and partly because her pulses already throbbed with that new life, whose misdirected energies produced, a few years afterwards, results so lamentable. Even now a people contending for their liberties awakened the sympathies of France. America had sent three Commissioners—one of whom was Benjamin Franklin—to Paris, to cultivate as opportunity offered the friendship of the French Government. For a time they laboured without visible results. But when news came that Burgoyne and his army had surrendered, hesitation was at an end. A treaty was signed by which France and America engaged to make common cause against England. The King opposed this treaty so long as he dared, but he was forced to give way. England, of course, accepted it as a declaration of war.

Spain could not miss the opportunity of avenging herself upon England. Her King desired to live at peace, he said, and to see his neighbours do the same. But he was profoundly interested in the liberties of the young Republic, and he was bound by strong ties to his good brother of France. Above all, England had in various quarters of the world grievously wronged him, by violating his territory and interfering with the trade of his subjects. And so he deemed it proper that he should waste the scanty substance of his people in equipping fleets and armies. When his preparations were complete he joined France and America in the league, and declared war against England.

The fleets of France and Spain appeared in the British Channel, and England had to face the perils of invasion. The spirit of her people rose nobly to meet the impending trial. The southern counties were one great camp. Voluntary contributions from all parts of the country aided Government to equip ships and soldiers. The King was to head his warlike people, should the enemy land, and share their danger and their glory. But the black cloud rolled harmlessly away, and the abounding heroism of the people was not further evoked. The invading admirals quarrelled. One of them wished to land at once; the other wished first to dispose of the English fleet. They could not agree upon a course, and therefore they sailed away home each to his own country, having effected nothing.

The war spread itself over a very wide surface. In the north, Paul Jones with three American ships alarmed the Scotch coast and destroyed much shipping. Spain besieged Gibraltar, but failed to regain that much-coveted prize. On the African coast the French took Senegal from the English, and the English took Goree from the French. In the West Indies the French took St. Vincent and Granada. On the American Continent, from New York to Savannah, the same wasteful and bloody labour was ruthlessly pursued.

The remaining years of the war were distinguished by few striking or decisive enterprises. The fleet sent by France sailed hither and thither in a feeble manner, accomplishing nothing. When General Howe was made aware of its approach, he abandoned Philadelphia and retired to New York. Washington followed him on his retreat, but neither then nor for some time afterwards could effect much. Congress and the American people formed sanguine expectations of the French alliance, and ceased to put forth the great efforts which distinguished the earlier period of the war. The English overran Georgia and the Carolinas. The Americans captured two or three forts. The war degenerated into a series of marauding expeditions. Some towns, innumerable farm-houses, were burned by the English.

Occasional massacres took place. With increasing frequency, prisoners were, under a variety of pretexts, put to death. On both sides feeling had become intensely bitter. On both sides cruelties of a most savage type were perpetrated.

To the very end Washington's army was miserably supplied, and endured extreme hardships. Congress was a weak, and, it must be added, a very unwise body. The ablest men were in the army, and Congress was composed of twenty or thirty persons of little character or influence. They had no authority to impose taxes. They tried to borrow money in Europe, and failed. They had only one resource—the issue of paper currency, and this was carried to such a wild excess that latterly a colonel's pay would not buy oats for his horse. Washington ceased to have the means of purchasing. Reluctantly, and under pressure of extreme necessity, he forcibly exacted supplies of meat and flour from the neighbourhood. Not otherwise could he save his army from dissolution and the country from ruin.

But there was one respect in which the cause grew constantly in strength. Men do not fight for eight years, in a war like this, without learning to hate each other. With a deep and deadly hatred the American people hated the power which ruthlessly inflicted upon them such cruel sufferings. Under the growing influence of this hatred, men became soldiers with increasing alacrity. The hardships of soldier-life no longer daunted them, so long as they had the English to resist. The trouble of short enlistments had ceased, and Washington was at length at the head of an army, often ill fed and always ill clad, but disciplined and invincibly resolved that their country should be free.

XII.

MAJOR ANDRÉ.

The Americans had a strong fortress at West Point, on the Hudson river. It was one of the most important places in the country, and its acquisition was anxiously desired by the English. Possession of West Point would have given them command of the Hudson, up which their ships of war could have sailed for more than a hundred miles. But that fort, sitting impregnably on rocks two hundred feet above the level of the river, was hard to win; and the Americans were careful to garrison effectively a position so vitally important.

In the American army was an officer named Arnold, who had served, not without distinction from the beginning of the war. He had fought in Canada when the Americans unsuccessfully invaded that province. His courage and skill had been conspicuous in the engagements which led to the surrender of Burgoyne. He was, however, a vain, reckless, unscrupulous person. He had by extravagance in living involved himself in debt, which he aggravated hopelessly by ill-judged mercantile speculations. He had influence with Washington to obtain the command of West Point. There is little doubt that when he sought the appointment it was with the full intention of selling that important fortress to the enemy. He opened negotiations at once with Sir Henry Clinton, then in command of the English army at New York.

Clinton sent Major André to arrange the terms of the contemplated treachery. A mournful interest attaches to the name of this young officer: the fate which befell him was so very sad. He was of French descent—high-spirited, accomplished, affectionate, merry-hearted. It was a service which a high-principled man would scarcely have coveted. But André desired eagerly to have the merit of gaining West Point, and he volunteered for this perilous enterprise.

At midnight Major André landed from the boat of a British ship of war, at a lonely place where Arnold waited him. Their conference lasted so long that it was deemed unsafe for André to return to the ship. He was conducted to a place of concealment within the American lines, to await the return of darkness. He completed his arrangement with Arnold, and received drawings of the betrayed fortress. His mission was now accomplished. The ship from which he had come lay full in view. Would that he could reach her! But difficulties arose, and it was resolved that he must ride to New York, a distance of fifty miles. Disguising himself as he best could, André reluctantly accepted this very doubtful method of escape from his fearful jeopardy.

Sept. 1780 A.D.

Within the American lines he had some narrow escapes, but the pass given by Arnold carried him through. He was at length beyond the lines. His danger might now be considered at an end, and he rode cheerfully on his lonely journey. He was crossing a small stream—thick woods on his right hand and his left enhanced the darkness of the night. Three armed men stepped suddenly from among the trees and ordered him to stand. From the dress of one of them, André thought he was among friends. He hastened to tell them he was a British officer, on very special business, and he must not be detained. Alas for poor Major André, they were not friends; and the dress which deceived him had been given to the man who wore it when he was a prisoner with the English, in place of a better garment of which his captors had stripped him.

André was searched; but at first nothing was found. It seemed as if he might yet be allowed to proceed, when one of the three men exclaimed, "Boys, I am not satisfied. His boots must come off." André's countenance fell. His boots were searched, and Arnold's drawings of West Point were discovered. The men knew then that he was a spy. He vainly offered them money. They were incorruptible. He was taken to the nearest military station, and the tidings were at once sent to Washington, who chanced to be then at West Point. Arnold had timely intimation of the disaster, and fled for refuge to a British ship of war.

André was tried by a court formed of officers of the American army. He gave a frank and truthful account of his part in the unhappy transaction—bringing into due prominence the circumstance that he was brought, without intention or knowledge on his part, within the American lines. The court judged him on his own statement, and condemned him to be hanged as a spy.

His capture and sentence caused deep sensation in the English army, and every effort was made to save him. But Washington was resolute that he should die. The danger to the patriot cause had been too great to leave any place for relenting. There were dark intimations of other treasons yet unrevealed. It was needful to give emphatic warning of the perils which waited on such unlawful negotiations. André begged that he might be allowed to die a soldier's death. Even this poor boon was refused to the unhappy young man. Since the awful lesson must be given, Washington considered that no circumstance fitted to enhance its terrors should be withheld. But this was mercifully concealed from André to the very last.

Ten days after his arrest, André was led forth to die. He

was under the impression that his last request had been granted, and that he would die by the bullet. It was a fresh pang when the gibbet, with its ghastly preparations, stood before him. "How hard is my fate," he said; "but it will soon be over." He bandaged his own eyes; with his own hands adjusted the noose to his neck. The cart on which he stood moved away, and poor Major André was no longer in the world of living men. Forty years afterwards his remains were brought home to England and laid in Westminster Abbey.

XIII.

THE CLOSE OF THE WAR.

During the later years of the war the English kept possession of the Southern States, which, as we have seen, they had gained so easily. When the last campaign opened, Lord Cornwallis with a strong force represented British authority in the South, and did all that he found possible for the suppression of the patriots. But the time was past when any real progress in that direction could be made. A certain vigorous and judicious General Greene, with such rough semblance of an army as he could draw together, gave Lord Cornwallis many rude shocks. The English gained little victories occasionally, but they suffered heavy losses, and the territory over which they held dominion was upon the whole becoming smaller.

1781 A.D.

About midsummer, the joyous news reached Washington that a powerful French fleet, with an army on board, was about to sail for America. With this reinforcement, Washington had it in his power to deliver a blow which would break the strength of the enemy, and hasten the close of the war. Clinton held New York, and Cornwallis was fortifying himself in Yorktown. The French fleet sailed for the Chesapeake, and Washington decided in consequence that his attack should be made on Lord Cornwallis. With all possible secrecy and speed the American troops were moved southwards to Virginia. They were joined by the French, and they stood before Yorktown a force 12,000 strong. Cornwallis had not expected them, and he called on Clinton to aid him. But it was too late. He was already in a grasp from which there was no escaping.

Throughout the war, the weakness of his force often obliged Washington to adopt a cautious and defensive policy, which grievously disappointed the expectations of his impatient countrymen. It is not therefore to be imagined that his leadership was wanting in vigour. Within his calm and well-balanced mind there lurked a fiery energy, ready to burst forth when occasion required. The siege of Yorktown was pushed on with extraordinary vehemence. The English, as their wont is, made a stout defence, and strove by desperate sallies to drive the assailants from their works. But in a few days the defences of Yorktown lay in utter ruin, beaten to the ground by the powerful artillery of the Americans. The English guns were silenced. The English shipping was fired by red-hot shot from the French batteries. Ammunition began to grow scarce. The place could not be held much longer, and Clinton still delayed his coming. Lord Cornwallis must either force his way out and escape to the North, or surrender. One night he began to embark his men in order to cross the York river and set out on his desperate march to New York. A violent storm arose and scattered his boats. The men who had embarked got back with difficulty, under fire from the American batteries. All hope was now at an end. In about a fortnight from the opening of the siege, the British army, 8000 strong, laid down its arms.

The joy of America over this great crowning success knew no bounds. One highly emotional patriot was said to have expired from mere excess of rapture. Some others lost their reason. In the army, all who were under arrest were at once set at liberty. A day of solemn thanksgiving was proclaimed and devoutly observed throughout the rejoicing States.

Well might the colonists rejoice, for their long and bitter

struggle was now about to close. Stubborn King George would not yield yet. But England and her Parliament were sick of this hopeless and inglorious war. The House of Commons voted that all who should advise the continuance of the war were enemies to the country. A new Ministry was formed, and negotiations with a view to peace were begun. The King had no doubt that if America were allowed to go, the West Indies would go—Ireland would go—all his foreign possessions would go; and discrowned England would sink into weakness and contempt. But too much heed had already been given to the King and his fancies. Peace was concluded with France and Spain, and the independence of America was at length recognized.

1782 A.D.

Jan. 20, 1783 A.D.

Eight years had passed since the first blood was shed at Lexington. Thus long the unyielding English, unused to failure, had striven to regain the lost ascendency. Thus long the colonists had borne the miseries of invasion, not shaken in their faith that the independence which they had undertaken to win was well worth all it cost them. And now they were free, and England was the same to them as all the rest of the world, —" in peace, a friend ; in war, a foe." They had little left them but their liberty and their soil. They had been unutterably devastated by those eight bloody years. Their fields had been wasted ; their towns had been burned. Commerce was extinct. Money had almost disappeared from the country. Their public debt reached the large sum of one hundred and seventy millions of dollars. The soldiers who had fought out the national independence were not paid till they showed some disposition to compel a settlement. There was nothing which could be called a Government. There were thirteen sovereign States, loosely knit together by a Congress. That body had power to discuss questions affecting the general good; to pass resolutions; to request the several States to give effect to these resolutions. The States might or might not comply with such request. Habitually they did not, especially when money was asked for. Congress had no power to tax. It merely apportioned among the States the amounts required for the public service, and each State was expected to levy a tax for its proportion. But in point of fact it became utterly impossible to get money by this process.

Great hardships were endured by the labouring population. The impatience of a suffering people expressed itself in occasional sputterings of insurrection. Two thousand men of Massachusetts rose in arms to demand that the collection of debts should be suspended. It was some weeks before that rising could be quelled, as the community generally sympathized with the insurgents. During four or five years the miseries of the ungoverned country seemed to warrant the belief that her war of independence had been a mistake.

1786
A.D.

But a future of unparalleled magnificence lay before this sorely vexed and discouraged people. The boundless corn-lands of the west, the boundless cotton-fields of the south, waited to yield their wealth. Pennsylvania held unimagined treasures of coal and iron—soon to be evoked by the irresistible spell of patient industry. America was a vast storehouse, prepared by the Great Father against the time when his children would have need of it. The men who are the stewards over its opulence have now freed themselves from some entanglements and hindrances which grievously diminished their efficiency, and stand prepared to enter in good earnest upon that high industrial vocation to which Providence has called them.

There had been periods during the war when confidence in Washington's leadership was shaken. He sustained many reverses. He oftentimes retreated. He adhered tenaciously to a defensive policy, when Congress and people were burning with impatience to inflict crushing defeat upon the foe. The deplorable insufficiency of his resources was overlooked, and the blame of every disaster fell on him. And when at length the cause began to prosper, and hope brightened into triumph, timid people were apt to fear that Washington was growing too powerful. He had become the idol of a great army. He had but to signify his readiness to accept a throne, and his soldiers would have crowned him King. It was usual in the revolutions of the world that a military chief should grasp at supreme power; and so it was feared that Washington was to furnish one example more of that lawless and vulgar lust of power by which human history has been so largely dishonoured.

But Washington sheathed his sword, and returned gladly to his home on the banks of the Potomac. He proposed to spend his days " in cultivating the affections of good men, and in the practice of the domestic virtues." He hoped " to glide gently down the stream which no human effort can ascend." He occupied himself with the care of his farm, and had no deeper feeling than thankfulness that he was at length eased of a load of public care. The simple grandeur of his character was now revealed beyond possibility of misconception. The measure of American veneration for this greatest of all Americans was full. Henceforth Mount Vernon was a shrine to which pilgrim feet were ever turned—evoking such boundless love and reverence as never were elsewhere exhibited on American soil.

XIV.

THE THIRTEEN STATES BECOME A NATION.

Washington saw from the beginning that his country was without a government. Congress was a mere name. There were still thirteen sovereign States—in league for the moment, but liable to be placed at variance by the differences which time would surely bring. Washington was satisfied that without a central government they could never be powerful or respected. Such a government, indeed, was necessary in order even to their existence. European powers would, in its absence, introduce dissensions among them. Men's minds would revert to that form of government with which they were familiar. Some ambitious statesman or soldier would make himself King, and the great experiment, based upon the equality of rights, would prove an ignominious failure.

The more sagacious Americans shared Washington's belief on this question. Conspicuous among these was Alexander Hamilton—perhaps, next to Washington, the greatest American of that age. Hamilton was a brave and skilful soldier, a brilliant debater, a persuasive writer, a wise statesman. In his nineteenth year he entered the army, at the very beginning of the war. The quick eye of Washington discovered the remarkable promise of the lad. He raised him to high command in the army, and afterwards to high office in the government. It was Hamilton who brought order out of the financial chaos which followed the war. It was Hamilton who suggested the convention to consider the framing of a new Constitution. Often, during the succeeding years, Hamilton's temperate and sagacious words calmed the storms which marked the infancy of the great Republic. His career had a dark and bloody close. In his forty-seventh year he stood face to face, one bright July morning, with a savage politician named Aaron Burr—a grandson of Jonathan Edwards the great divine. Burr had fastened a quarrel upon him, in the hope of murdering him in a duel. Hamilton had resolved not to fire. Burr fired with careful aim, and Hamilton fell, wounded to death. One of the ablest men America has ever possessed was thus lost to her.

1804 A.D.

Immediately after the close of the war, Hamilton began to discuss the weakness of the existing form of government. He was deeply convinced that the union of the States, in order to be lasting, must be established on a solid basis; and his writings did much to spread this conviction among his fellow-countrymen. Washington never ceased from his retirement to urge the same views. Gradually the urgent need of a better system was recognized. It indeed soon became too obvious to be denied. Congress found it utterly impossible to get money. Between 1781 and 1786, ten millions of dollars were called for from the States, but only two millions and a half were obtained. The interest on the debt was unpaid. The ordinary expenses of the government were unprovided for. The existing form of government was an acknowledged failure. Something better had to be devised, or the tie which bound the thirteen States would be severed.

1783 A.D.

Hamilton obtained the sanction of Congress to his proposal that a convention of delegates from the several States should be held. This convention was to review the whole subject of the governing arrangement, and to recommend such alterations as should be considered adequate to the exigencies of the time. Philadelphia, as usual, was

1787 A.D.

the place of meeting. Thither, in the month of May, came the men who were charged with the weighty task of framing a government under which the thirteen States should become a nation.

Fifty-five men composed this memorable council. Among them were the wisest men of whom America, or perhaps any other country, could boast. Washington himself presided. Benjamin Franklin brought to this—his latest and his greatest task—the ripe experience of eighty-two years. New York sent Hamilton—regarding whom Prince Talleyrand said, long afterwards, that he had known nearly all the leading men of his time, but he had never known one on the whole equal to Hamilton. With these came many others whose names are held in enduring honour. Since the meeting of that first Congress which pointed the way to independence, America had seen no such assembly.

The convention sat for four months. The great work which occupied it divided the country into two parties. One party feared most the evils which arise from weakness of the governing power, and sought relief from these in a close union of the States under a strong government. Another party dwelt more upon the miserable condition of the over-governed nations of Europe, and feared the creation of a government which might grow into a despotism. The aim of the one was to vest the largest possible measure of power in a central government. Hamilton, indeed—to whom the British Constitution seemed the most perfect on earth—went so far as to desire that the States should be merely great municipalities, attending only, like an English corporation, to their own local concerns. The aim of the other was to circumscribe the powers accorded to the general government—to vindicate the sovereignty of the individual States, and give to it the widest possible scope. These two sets of opinions continued to exist and conflict for three-quarters of a century, till that which assigned an undue dominion to what were called State Rights, perished in the overthrow of the great Rebellion.

Slowly and through endless debate the convention worked out its plan of a government. The scheme was submitted to Congress, and thence sent down to the several States. Months of fiery discussion ensued. Somewhat reluctantly, by narrow majorities, in the face of vehement protests, the Constitution was at length adopted under which the thirteen States were to become so great.

Great Britain has no written Constitution. She has her laws; and it is expected that all future laws shall be in tolerable harmony with the principles on which her past legislation has been founded. But if Parliament were to enact, and the Sovereign to sanction, any law at variance with these principles, there is no help for it. Queen, Lords, and Commons are our supreme authority, from whose decisions there lies no appeal. In America it is different. There the supreme authority is a written Constitution. Congress may unanimously enact, and the President may cordially sanction, a new law. Two or three judges, sitting in the same building where Congress meets, may compare that law with the Constitution. If it is found at variance with the Constitution, it is unceremoniously declared to be no law, and entitled to no man's obedience. With a few alterations, this Constitution remains in full force now—gathering around it, as it increases in age, the growing reverence of the people. The men who framed it must have been very wise. The people for whom it was framed must possess in high degree the precious Anglo-Saxon veneration for law. Otherwise the American paper Constitution must long ago have shared the fate of the numerous documents of this class under which the French vainly sought rest during their first Revolution.

Each of the thirteen States was sovereign, and the government of America hitherto had been merely a league of independent powers. Now the several States parted with a certain amount of their sovereignty, and vested it in a General Government. The General Government was to levy taxes, to coin money, to regulate commercial relations with foreign countries, to establish post-offices and post-roads, to establish courts of law, to declare war, to raise and maintain armies and navies, to make treaties, to borrow money on the credit of the United States. The individual States expressly relinquished the right to perform these sovereign functions.

These powers were intrusted to two Houses of Legislation and a President. The House of Representatives is composed of two hundred and forty-three members. The members hold their seats for two years, and are paid five thousand dollars annually. Black men and Indians were not allowed to vote; but all white men had a voice in the election of their representatives. To secure perfect equality of representation, members are distributed according to population. Thus, in 1863 a member was given to every 124,000 inhabitants. Every ten years a readjustment takes place, and restores the equality which the growth of the intervening period has disturbed.

The large States send necessarily a much larger number of members to the Lower House than the small States do. Thus New York sends thirty-one, while Rhode Island sends only two, Delaware and Florida only one. The self-love of the smaller States was wounded by an arrangement which resembled absorption into the larger communities. The balance was redressed in the constitution of the Upper Chamber—the Senate. That body is composed of seventy-six members, elected by the legislatures of the States. Every State, large or small, returns two members. The small States were overborne in the Lower House, but in the Senate they enjoyed an importance equal to that of their most populous neighbours. The senators are elected for six years, and are paid at the same rate as the members of the House of Representatives.

The head of the American Government is the President. He holds office for four years. Each State chooses a number of persons equal to the total number of members whom it returns to the Houses of Legislation. These persons elect the President. They elect also a Vice-President, lest the President should be removed by death or otherwise during his term of office. All laws enacted by Congress must be submitted to the President. He may refuse to pass them—sending them back with a statement of his objections. But should both Houses, by a vote of two-thirds of their number, adhere to the rejected measures, they become law in spite of the President's veto. The President appoints his own Cabinet Ministers, and these have no seats in Congress. Their annual reports upon the affairs of their departments are communicated to Congress by the President, along with his own Message. The President is Commander-in-Chief of the Army and Navy. With concurrence of the Senate, he appoints ambassadors, judges of the Supreme Court, and other public officers.

Every State has a government after the same pattern, composed of two Houses of Legislation and a Governor. These authorities occupy themselves with the management of such affairs as exclusively concern their own State, and have, therefore, not been relinquished to the General Government. They legislate in regard to railway and other public companies. They see to the administration of justice within their own territory, unless in the case of crimes committed against the Government. They pass such laws as are required in regard to private property and rights of succession. Above all, they retain all the powers of which they were ever possessed in regard to slavery. The Constitution gave Congress authority to suppress the importation of slaves after the year 1808. Not otherwise was the slave-question interfered with. That remained wholly under the control of the individual States.

But the men who framed this Constitution, however wise, were liable to err. And if they were found in after years to have erred, what provision—other than a revolution—was made for correcting their mistakes? A very simple and very effective one. When two-thirds of both Houses of Legislation deem it necessary that some amendment of the Constitution should be made, they propose it to the legislatures of the several States. When three-fourths of these judicatories adopt the proposal, it becomes a part of the Constitution. There have been in all fifteen amendments adopted, most of them very soon after the Constitution itself came into existence.

And now the conditions of the great experiment are adjusted. Three millions of Americans have undertaken to govern themselves. Europe does not believe that any people can prosper in such an undertaking. Europe still clings to the belief that, in every country, a few Heaven-sent families must guide the destinies of the incapable, child-like millions. America—having no faith in Heaven-sent families—believes that the millions are the best and safest guides of their own destinies, and means to act on that belief. On her success great issues wait. If the Americans show that they can govern themselves, all the other nations will gradually put their hands to the same ennobling work.

The first step to be taken under the new Constitution was to elect a President. There was but one man who was thought of for this high and untried office. George Washington was unanimously chosen. Congress was summoned to meet in New York on the 4th of March. But the

1789 A.D.

members had to travel far on foot, or on horseback. Roads were bad, bridges were few; streams, in that spring-time, were swollen. It was some weeks after the appointed time before business could be commenced.

That Congress had difficult work to do, and it was done patiently, with much plain sense and honesty. As yet there was no revenue. Everywhere there was debt. The General Government had debt, and each of the States had debt. There was the Foreign Debt—due to France, Holland, and Spain. There was the Army Debt—for arrears of pay and pensions. There was the Debt of the Five Great Departments—for supplies obtained during the war. There was a vast issue of paper money to be redeemed. There were huge arrears of interest. And, on the other hand, there was no provision whatever for these enormous obligations.

Washington, with a sigh, asked a friend, "What is to be done about this heavy debt?" "There is but one man in America can tell you," said his friend, "and that is Alexander Hamilton." Washington made Hamilton Secretary to the Treasury. The success of his financial measures was immediate and complete. "He smote the rock of the national resources," said Daniel Webster, "and abundant streams of revenue gushed forth. He touched the dead corpse of the public credit, and it sprang upon its feet." All the war debts of the States were assumed by the General Government. Efficient provision was made for the regular payment of interest, and for a sinking fund to liquidate the principal. Duties were imposed on shipping, on goods imported from abroad, and on spirits manufactured at home. The vigour of the Government inspired public confidence. Commerce began to revive. In a few years the American flag was seen on every sea. The simple manufactures of the country resumed their long interrupted activity. A National Bank was established. Courts were set up, and judges were appointed. The salaries of the President and the great functionaries were settled. A home was chosen for the General Government on the banks of the Potomac; where the capital of the Union was to supplant the little wooden village—remote from the agitations which arise in the great centres of population. Innumerable details connected with the establishment of a new government were discussed and fixed. Novel as the circumstances were, little of the work then done has required to be undone. Succeeding generations of Americans have approved the wisdom of their early legislators, and continue unaltered the arrangements which were framed at the outset of the national existence.

Thirty years of peace succeeded the War of Independence. There were, indeed, passing troubles with the Indians, ending always in the sharp chastisement of those disagreeable savages.

1804 A.D. There was an expedition against Tripoli, to avenge certain indignities which the barbarians of that region had offered to American shipping. There was a misunderstanding with the French Directory, which was carried to a

1789 A.D. somewhat perilous extreme. A desperate fight took place between a French frigate and an American frigate, resulting in the surrender of the former. But these trivial agitations did not disturb the profound tranquillity of the nation, or hinder its progress in that career of prosperity on which it had now entered.

Washington was President during the first eight years of the Constitution. He survived his withdrawal from public life only

1799 A.D. three years, dying, after a few hours' illness, in the sixty-eighth year of his age. His countrymen mourned him with a sorrow sincere and deep. Their reverence for him has not diminished with the progress of the years. Each new generation of Americans catches up the veneration—calm, intelligent, but profound—with which its fathers regarded the blameless Chief. To this day there is an affectionate watchfulness for opportunities to express the honour in which his name is held. To this day the steamers which ply upon the Potomac strike mournful notes upon the bell as they sweep past Mount Vernon, where Washington spent the happiest days of his life, and where he died.

XV.

THE WAR WITH GREAT BRITAIN.

AMERICA was well contented during many years to be merely a spectator of the Great European War. In spite of some differences which had arisen, she still cherished a kindly feeling towards France—her friend in the old time of need. She had still a bitter hatred to England, her tyrant, as she deemed, and her cruel foe. But her sympathies did not regulate her policy. She had no call to avenge the dishonour offered to royalty by the people of France. As little was it her business to strengthen France against the indignation of outraged monarchs. Her distance exempted her from taking any part in the bloody politics of Europe, and she was able to look quietly on while the flames of war consumed the nations of the Old World. Her ships enjoyed a monopoly. She traded impartially with all the combatants. The energies of Europe were taxed to the uttermost by a gigantic work of mutual destruction. The Americans conveyed to the people thus unprofitably occupied the foreign articles of which they stood in need, and made great gain of their neighbours' madness.

But the time came when France and England were to put forth efforts more gigantic than before, to compass the ruin of each other. England gave out a decree announcing that all the coasts of France and her allies were in a state of blockade, and that any vessels attempting to trade with the blockaded countries were liable to seizure. At that

1806
A.D.

time nearly all the Continent was in alliance with France. Napoleon replied by declaring the British Islands in a state of blockade. These decrees closed Europe against American vessels. Many captures were made, especially by English cruisers. American merchants suffered grievous losses, and loudly expressed their just wrath against the wicked laws which wrought them so much evil.

There was another question out of which mischief arose. England has always maintained that any person who has once been her subject can never cease to be so. He may remove to another country. He may become the citizen of another state. English law recognizes no such transaction. England claims that the man is still an English subject—entitled to the advantages of that relation, and bound by its obligations. America, on the other hand, asserted that men could lay down their original citizenship, and assume another—could transfer their allegiance—could relinquish the privileges and absolve themselves from the obligations which they inherited. The Englishmen who settled on her soil were regarded by her as American citizens and as nothing else.

Circumstances arose which bestowed dangerous importance upon these conflicting doctrines. England at that time obtained sailors by impressment. That is to say, she seized men who were engaged on board merchant vessels, and compelled them to serve on board her ships of war. It was a process second only to the slave-trade in its iniquity. The service to which men were thus introduced could not but be hateful. There was a copious desertion, as opportunity offered, and America was the natural refuge. English ships of war claimed the right to search American vessels for men who had deserted; and also for men who, as born English subjects, were liable to be impressed. It may well be believed that this right was not always exercised with a strict regard to justice. It was not always easy to distinguish an Englishman from an American. Perhaps the

English captains were not very scrupulous as to the evidence on which they acted. The Americans asserted that six thousand men, on whom England had no shadow of claim, were ruthlessly carried off to fight under a flag they hated; the English Government admitted the charge to the extent of sixteen hundred men. The American people vehemently resented the intolerable pretension of England. Occasionally an American ship resisted it, and blood was freely shed.

When England and France decreed the closing of all European ports against commerce, America hastened to show that she could be as unwise as her neighbours. Congress prohibited commerce with the European powers which had so offended. The people, wiser than their rulers, disapproved this measure, but the Government enforced it. The President was empowered to call out militia and employ armed vessels to prevent cargoes of American produce from leaving the country. It was hoped that England and France, thus bereaved of articles which were deemed necessary, would be constrained to repeal their injurious decrees.

1807
A.D.

Thus for four years commerce was suspended, and grass grew on the idle wharves of New York and Philadelphia. The cotton and tobacco of the Southern States, the grain and timber of the North, were stored up to await the return of reason to the governing powers of the world. Tens of thousands of working people were thrown idle. The irritation of the impoverished nation was fast ripening towards war.

America wanted now the wise leadership which she enjoyed at the period of her revolutionary struggle. Washington had never ceased to urge upon his countrymen the desirableness of being on good terms with England. But Washington was dead, and his words were not remembered. Franklin was dead. Hamilton had fallen by the murdering hand of Aaron Burr. There was a strong party eager for war. The commercial towns on the sea-bord dreaded the terrible ships of England, and desired to negotiate for redress of grievances. The people of the interior, having no towns to be bombarded, preferred to try their strength with England in battle. Some attempts at negotiation resulted in failure. At length Congress ended suspense by passing a Bill which declared war against Great Britain.

June 18, 1812 A.D.

It was a bolder challenge than America supposed it to be. England, indeed, had her hands full. The power of her great foe seemed to be irresistible. But even then the axe was laid to its roots. In that same month of June Napoleon crossed the river Niemen and entered Russia upon his fatal march to Moscow. A few weeks before, the Duke of Wellington had wrenched from his grasp the two great frontier fortresses of Spain, and was now beginning to drive the French armies out of the Peninsula. England would soon have leisure for her new assailant. But all this was as yet unseen.

When war was declared, England possessed one thousand ships of war, and America possessed twenty. Their land forces were in like proportion. England had nearly a million of men under arms. America had an army reckoned at twenty-four thousand, many of them imperfectly disciplined and not yet to be relied upon in the field. Her treasury was empty. She was sadly wanting in officers of experience. She had declared war, but it was difficult to see what she could do in the way of giving effect to her hostile purposes.

But she held to these purposes with unfaltering tenacity. Four days after Congress had resolved to fight, England repealed those blockading decrees which had so justly offended the Americans. There remained now only the question of the right of search. The British Minister at Washington proposed that an attempt should be made to settle peaceably this sole remaining ground of quarrel. The proposal was declined. The

American war party would not swerve from its unhappy determination.

The first efforts of the Americans were signally unsuccessful. They attacked Canada with an army of 2500 men. But this force had scarcely got upon Canadian ground when it was driven back. It was besieged in Fort Detroit by an inferior British army and forced to surrender. The unfortunate General Hull, who commanded, was brought to trial by his angry countrymen and sentenced to be shot. He was pardoned, however, in consideration of former services.

August, 1812 A.D.

A second invasion followed, closed by a second surrender. During other two campaigns the Americans prosecuted their invasion. Ships were built and launched upon the great lakes which lie between the territories of the combatants. Sea-fights were fought, in one of which the American triumph was so complete that all the British vessels surrendered. Many desperate engagements took place on shore. Some forts were captured. Some towns were burned. Many women and children were made homeless. Many brave men were slain. But the invaders made no progress. Everywhere the Canadians, with the help of the regular troops, were able to hold their own. It was a coarse method of solving the question which was in dispute between the countries, and it was utterly fruitless.

At sea a strange gleam of good fortune cheered the Americans. It was there England felt herself omnipotent. She, with her thousand ships, might pardonably despise the enemy who came against her with twenty. But it was there disaster overtook her.

During the autumn months a series of encounters took place between single British and American ships. In every instance victory remained with the Americans. Five English vessels were taken or destroyed. The Americans were in most of these engagements more heavily

1812 A.D.

manned and armed than their enemies. But the startling fact remained. Five British ships of war had been taken in battle by the Americans. Five defeats had been sustained by England. Her sovereignty of the sea had received a rude shock.

The loss of a great battle would not have moved England more profoundly than the capture of these five unimportant ships. It seemed to many to foretell the downfall of her maritime supremacy. She had ruled the seas because, heretofore, no other country produced sailors equal to hers. But a new power had now arisen, whose home, equally with that of Britannia herself, was upon the deep. If America could achieve these startling successes while she had only twenty ships, what might she not accomplish with that ampler force which she would hereafter possess? England had many enemies, all of whom rejoiced to see in these defeats the approaching decay of her envied greatness.

Among English sailors there was a burning eagerness to wipe out the unlooked-for disgrace which had fallen upon the flag. A strict blockade of American ports was maintained. On board the English ships which cruised on the American coasts impatient search was made for opportunities of retrieving the honour of the service.

Two English ships lay off Boston in the summer of 1813, under the command of Captain Broke. Within the bay the American frigate *Chesapeake* had lain for many months. Captain Broke had bestowed especial pains upon the training of his men, and he believed he had made them a match for any equal force. He and they vehemently desired to test their prowess in battle. He sent away one of his ships, retaining only the *Shannon*, which was slightly inferior to the *Chesapeake* in guns and in men. And then he stood close in to the shore, and sent to Captain Lawrence of the *Chesapeake* an invitation to come forth that they might "try the fortune of their respective flags."

From his mast-head Captain Broke watched anxiously the movements of the hostile ship. Soon he saw her canvas shaken out to the breeze. His challenge was accepted. The stately *Chesapeake* moved slowly down the bay, attended by many barges and pleasure-boats. To the over-sanguine men of Boston it seemed that Captain Lawrence sailed out to assured victory. They crowded to house-top and hill to witness his success. They prepared a banquet to celebrate his triumphant return.

Slowly and in grim silence the hostile ships drew near. No shot was fired till they were within a stone-throw of each other, and the men in either could look into the faces of those they were about to destroy. Then began the horrid carnage of a sea-fight. The well-trained British fired with steady aim, and every shot told. The rigging of their enemy was speedily ruined; her stern was beaten in; her decks were swept by discharges of heavy guns loaded with musket-balls. The American firing was greatly less effective. After a few broadsides, the ships came into contact. The *Shannon* continued to fire grape-shot from two of her guns. The *Chesapeake* could now reply feebly, and only with musketry. Captain Broke prepared to board. Over decks heaped with slain and slippery with blood the Englishmen sprang upon the yielding foe. The American flag was pulled down, and resistance ceased.

June 1, 1813 A.D.

The fight lasted but a quarter of an hour. So few minutes ago the two ships, peopled by seven hundred men in the pride of youth and strength, sailed proudly over seas which smiled in the peaceful sunlight of that summer evening. Now their rigging lies in ruins upon the cumbered decks; their sides are riven by shot; seventy-one dead bodies wait to be thrown overboard; one hundred and fifty-seven men lie wounded and in anguish—some of them to die, some to recover and live out cheerless lives, till the grave opens for their mutilated and disfigured forms. Did these men hate each other with a hatred so intense that they could do no less than inflict these evils upon each other? They had no hatred at all. Their Governments differed, and this was their method of ascertaining who was in the right! Surely men will one day be wise enough to adopt some process for the adjustment of differences less wild in its inaccuracy, less brutish in its cruelty than this.

This victory, so quickly won and so decisive, restored the confidence of England in her naval superiority. The war went on with varying fortune. The Americans, awakening to the greatness of the necessity, put forth vigorous efforts to increase both army and navy. Frequent encounters between single ships occurred. Sometimes the American ship captured or destroyed the British. More frequently now the British ship captured or destroyed the American. The superb fighting capabilities of the race were splendidly illustrated, but no results of a more solid character can be enumerated.

But meanwhile momentous changes had occurred in Europe. Napoleon had been overthrown, and England was enjoying the brief repose which his residence in Elba afforded. She could bestow some attention now upon her American quarrel. Several regiments of Wellington's soldiers were sent to America, under the command of General Ross, and an attack upon Washington was determined. The force at General Ross's disposal was only 3500 men. With means so inconsiderable, it seemed rash to attack the capital of a great nation. But the result proved that General Ross had not underestimated the difficulties of the enterprise.

1814
A.D.

The Americans utterly failed in the defence of their capital. They were forewarned of the attack, and had good time to prepare. The militia of Pennsylvania and Virginia had promised their services, but were not found when they were needed. Only 7000 men could be drawn together to resist the advance of the English. These took post at Bladensburg, where there was a bridge over the Potomac. The English were greatly less numerous, but they were veterans who had fought under Wellington in many battles. To them it was play to rout the undisciplined American levies. They dashed upon the enemy, who, scarcely waiting to fire a shot, broke and fled towards Washington in hopeless confusion.

That same evening the British marched quietly into Washington. General Ross had orders to destroy or hold to ransom all public buildings. He offered to spare the national property, if a certain sum of money were paid to him. The authorities declined his proposal. Next day a great and most unjustifiable ruin was wrought. The Capitol, the President's residence, the Government offices, even the bridge over the Potomac—all were destroyed. The Navy-yard and Arsenal, with some ships in course of building, were set on fire by the Americans themselves. The President's house was pillaged by the soldiers before it was burned. These devastations were effected in obedience to peremptory orders from the British Government, on whom rests the shame of proceedings so reprehensible and so unusual in the annals of civilized war. On the same day the British withdrew from the ruins of the burning capital, and retired towards the coast.

The Americans were becoming weary of this unmeaning war. Hope of success there was none, now that Britain had no other enemy to engage her attention. America had no longer a ship of war to protect her coasts from insult. Her trade was extinct. Her exports, which were fourteen millions sterling before the war, had sunk to one-tenth of that amount. Two-thirds of the trading classes were insolvent. Most of the trading ships were taken. The revenue hitherto derived from customs had utterly ceased. The credit of the country was not good, and loans could not be obtained. Taxation became very oppressive, and thus enhanced extremely the unpopularity of the war. Some of the New England States refused to furnish men or money, and indicated a disposition to make peace for themselves, if they could not obtain it otherwise.

Peace was urgently needed, and happily was near at hand. Late one Saturday night a British sloop-of-war arrived at New York bearing a treaty of peace, already ratified by the British Government. The cry of "Peace! peace!" rang through the gladdened streets. The city burst into spontaneous illumination. The news reached Boston on Monday morning. Boston was almost beside herself with joy. A multitude of idle ships had long lain at her wharves. Before night carpenters were at work making them ready to go to sea. Sailors were engaged; cargoes were being passed on board. Boston returned without an hour's delay to her natural condition of commercial activity.

Feb. 11, 1815 A.D.

British and American Commissioners had met at Ghent, and had agreed upon terms of peace. The fruitlessness of war is a familiar discovery when men have calmness to review its losses and its gains. Both countries had endured much during these three years of hostilities; and now the peace left as they had been before the questions whose settlement was the object of the war.

The treaty was concluded on the 24th December. Could the news have been flashed by telegraph across the Atlantic, much brave life would have been saved. But seven weeks elapsed before it was known in the southern parts of America that the two countries were at peace. And meanwhile one of the bloodiest fights of the war had been fought.

1814 A.D.

New Orleans—a town of nearly 20,000 inhabitants—was

then, as it is now, one of the great centres of the cotton trade, and commanded the navigation of the Mississippi. The capture of a city so important could not fail to prove a heavy blow to America. An expedition for this purpose was organized. Just when the Commissioners at Ghent were felicitating themselves upon the peace they had made, the British army, in storm and intolerable cold, was being rowed on shore within a few miles of New Orleans.

Sir Edward Pakenham, one of the heroes of the Peninsula, commanded the English. The defence of New Orleans was intrusted to General Jackson. Jackson had been a soldier from his thirteenth year. He had spent a youth of extraordinary hardship. He was now a strong-willed, experienced, and skilful leader, in whom his soldiers had boundless confidence. Pakenham, fresh from the triumphs of the Peninsula, looked with mistaken contempt upon his formidable enemy.

Jackson's line of defence was something over half a mile in length. The Mississippi covered his right flank, an impassable swamp and jungle secured his left. Along his front ran a deep broad ditch, topped by a rampart composed of bales of cotton. In this strong position the Americans waited the coming of the enemy.

1815 A.D. At daybreak on the 8th January the British, 6000 strong, made their attack. The dim morning light revealed to the Americans the swift advance of the red-coated host. A murderous fire of grape and round-shot was opened from the guns mounted on the bastion. Brave men fell fast, but the assailants passed on through the storm. They reached the American works. It was their design to scale the ramparts, and, once within, to trust to their bayonets, which had never deceived them yet. But at the foot of the ramparts it was found that scaling-ladders had been omitted in the preparations for the assault! The men mounted on each other's shoulders, and thus some of them forced their way into the works, only to be shot down by the American riflemen. All was vain. A deadly fire streamed incessant from that fatal parapet upon the defenceless men below. Sir Edward Pakenham fell mortally wounded. The carnage was frightful, and the enterprise visibly hopeless. The troops were withdrawn in great confusion, having sustained a loss of 2000 men. The Americans had seven men killed and the same number wounded.

Thus closed the war. Both countries look with just pride upon the heroic courage so profusely displayed in battle, and upon the patient endurance with which great sacrifices were submitted to. It is pity these high qualities did not find a more worthy field for their exercise. The war was a gigantic folly and wickedness, such as no future generation, we may venture to hope, will ever repeat.

On the Fourth of July 1826 all America kept holiday. On that day fifty years ago the Declaration of Independence was signed, and America began her great career as a free country. Better occasion for jubilee the world has seldom known. The Americans must needs do honour to the Fathers of their Independence, most of whom have already passed away; two of whom —John Adams and Thomas Jefferson—died on this very day. They must pause and look back upon this amazing half century. The world had never seen growth so rapid. There were three millions of Americans who threw off the British yoke. Now there were twelve millions. The thirteen States had increased to twenty-four. The territory of the Union had been prodigiously enlarged. Louisiana had been sold by France. Florida had been ceded by Spain. Time after time tribes of vagrant Indians yielded up their lands and enrolled themselves subjects of the Great Republic. The Gulf of Mexico now bounded the Union

1803
A.D.

1820
A.D.

on the south, and the lakes which divide her from Canada on the north. From the Atlantic on the east, she already looked out upon the Pacific on the west. Canals had been cut leading from the great lakes to the Hudson, and the grain which grew on the corn-lands of the west, thousands of miles away, was brought easily to New York. Innumerable roads had been made. The debt incurred in the War of Independence had been all paid; and the still heavier debt incurred in the second war with England was being rapidly extinguished. A steady tide of emigration flowed westward. Millions of acres of the fertile wilderness which lay towards the setting sun had been at length made profitable to mankind. Extensive manufactories had been established in which cotton and woollen fabrics were produced. The foreign trade of the country amounted to forty millions sterling.

The Marquis Lafayette, now an old man, came to see once more before he died the country he had helped to save, and took part with wonder in the national rejoicing. The poor colonists, for whose liberties he fought, had already become a powerful and wealthy nation. Everywhere there had been expansion. Everywhere there were comfort and abundance. Everywhere there were boundless faith in the future, and a vehement, unresting energy, which would surely compel the fulfilment of any expectations, however vast.

BOOK III.

I.

KING COTTON.

When Europeans first visited the southern parts of America, they found in abundant growth there a plant destined to such eminence in the future history of the world as no other member of the vegetable family ever attained. It was an unimportant-looking plant, two or three feet in height, studded with pods somewhat larger than a walnut. In the appropriate season these pods opened, revealing a wealth of soft white fibre, embedded in which lay the seeds of the plant. This was Cotton. It was not unknown to the Old World. The Romans used cotton fabrics before the Christian era. India did so from a still remoter period. But the extent to which its use had been carried was trivial. Men clothed themselves as they best might in linen or woollen cloth, or simply in the skins of the beasts which they slew. The time was now at hand when an ampler provision for their wants was to be disclosed to them. Socially and politically, cotton has deeply influenced the course of human affairs. The mightiest conquerors sink into insignificance in presence of King Cotton.

The English began to cultivate a little cotton very soon after their settlement in America. But it was a difficult crop for them to handle. The plants grew luxuriantly. When autumn came the opening pods revealed a most satisfying opulence. The quantity of cotton produced excited the wonder of the planters. But the seeds of the plant adhered tenaciously to the fibre. Before the fibre could be used the seeds had to be removed. This was a slow and therefore a costly process. It was as much as a man could do in a day to separate one pound of cotton from the seeds. Cotton could never be abundant or cheap while this was the case.

But in course of time things came to pass in England which made it indispensable that cotton should be both abundant and cheap. In 1768 Richard Arkwright invented a machine for spinning cotton vastly superior to anything hitherto in use. Next year a greater than he—James Watt—announced a greater invention—his Steam Engine. England was ready now to begin her great work of weaving cotton for the world. But where was the cotton to be found?

Three or four years before Watt patented his Engine, and Arkwright his Spinning-frame, there was born in a New England farm-house a boy whose work was needed to complete theirs. His name was Eli Whitney. Eli was a born mechanic. It was a necessity of his nature to invent and construct. As a mere boy he made nails, pins, and walking-canes by novel processes, and thus earned money to support himself at college. In 1792 he went to Georgia to visit Mrs. Greene, the widow of that General Greene who so troubled Lord Cornwallis in the closing years of the war. In that primitive society, where few of the comforts of civilized life were yet enjoyed, no visits were so like those of the angels as the visits of a skilful mechanic. Eli constructed marvellous amusements for Mrs. Greene's children. He overcame all household difficulties by some ingenious contrivance. Mrs. Greene learned to wonder at him, and to believe nothing was impossible for him. One day Mrs. Greene entertained a party of her neighbours. The conversation turned upon the sorrows of the Planter. That unhappy tenacity with which the seeds of cotton adhered to the fibre was elaborately bemoaned. With an urgent demand from England for cotton, with boundless lands which grew nothing so well as cotton, it was hard to be so utterly baffled.

Mrs. Greene had unlimited faith in her friend Eli. She begged him to invent a machine which should separate the seeds of cotton from the fibre. Eli was of Northern upbringing, and had never even seen cotton in seed. He walked in to Savannah, and there, with some trouble, obtained a quantity of uncleaned cotton. He shut himself up in his room and brooded over the difficulty which he had undertaken to conquer.

All that winter Eli laboured—devising, hammering, building up, rejecting, beginning afresh. He had no help. He could not even get tools to buy, but had to make them with his own hands. At length his machine was completed, rude-looking, but visibly effective. Mrs. Greene invited the leading men of the State to her house. She conducted them in triumph to the building in which the machine stood. The owners of unprofitable cotton lands looked on with a wild flash of hope lighting up their desponding hearts. Possibilities of untold wealth to each of them lay in that clumsy structure. The machine was put in motion. It was evident to all that it could perform the work of hundreds of men. Eli had gained a great victory for mankind. In that rude log-hut of Georgia, Cotton was crowned King, and a new era opened for America and the world.

Ten years after Whitney's Cotton-gin was invented a huge addition was made to the cotton-growing districts of America. In 1803 Europe enjoyed a short respite from the mad Napoleon wars. France had recently acquired from Spain vast regions bordering on the Gulf of Mexico, and stretching far up the valley of the Mississippi, and westward to the Pacific. It was certain that peace in Europe would not last long. It was equally certain that when war was resumed France could not hold these possessions against the fleets of England. America wished to acquire, and was willing to pay for them. It was better to sell to the Americans, and equip soldiers with the price, than wait till England was ready to conquer. Napoleon sold, and America added Louisiana to her vast possessions.

Mark well these two events—the invention of a machine for cheaply separating the seeds of cotton from the fibre, and the purchase of Louisiana from the French. Out of those events flows the American history of the next half century. Not any other event since the War of Independence—not all other events put together, have done so much to shape and determine the career of the American people.

II.

SLAVERY.

When America gained her independence slavery existed in all the colonies. No State was free from the taint. Even the New England Puritans held slaves. At an early period they had learned to enslave their Indian neighbours. The children of the Pilgrims owned Indians, and in due time owned Africans, without remorse. But the number of slaves in the North was always small. At first it was not to the higher principle or clearer intelligence of the Northern men that this limited prevalence of slavery was due. The North was not a region where slave labour could ever be profitable. The climate was harsh, the soil rocky and bleak. Labour required to be directed by intelligence. In that comparatively unproductive land the mindless and heartless toil of the slave would scarcely defray the cost of his support. At the Revolution there were half a million of slaves in the colonies, and of these only thirty to forty thousand were in the North.

It was otherwise in the sunny and luxuriant South. The African was at home there, for the climate was like his own. The rich soil yielded its wealth to labour in the slightest and least intelligent form. The culture of rice, and tobacco, and cotton supplied the very kind of work which a slave was fitted to perform. The South found profitable employment for as many Africans as the slave-traders were able to steal.

And yet at the Revolution slavery enjoyed no great degree of favour. The free spirit enkindled by the war was in violent opposition to the existence of a system of bondage. The presence of the slaves had disabled the South from taking the part she ought in the War of Independence. The white men had to stay at home to watch the black. Virginia, Washington's State, furnished a reasonable proportion of troops; but the other Southern States were almost worthless. Everywhere in the North slavery was regarded as an objectionable and decaying institution. The leaders of the Revolution, themselves mainly slave-owners, were eagerly desirous that slavery should be abolished. Washington was utterly opposed to the system, and provided in his will for the emancipation of his own slaves. Hamilton was a member of an association for the gradual abolition of slavery. John Adams would never own a slave. Franklin, Patrick Henry, Madison, Munroe, were united in their reprobation of slavery. Jefferson, a Virginian, who prepared the Declaration of Independence, said that in view of slavery "he trembled for his country, when he reflected that God was just."

In the convention which met to frame a Constitution for America the feeling of antagonism to slavery was supreme. Had the majority followed their own course, provision would have been made then for the gradual extinction of slavery. But there arose here a necessity for one of those compromises by which the history of America has been so sadly marked. When it was proposed to prohibit the importation of slaves, all the Northern and most of the Southern States favoured the proposal. But South Carolina and Georgia were insatiable in their thirst for African labour. They decisively refused to become parties to a union in which there was to be no importation of slaves. The other States yielded. Instead of an immediate abolition of this hateful traffic, it was agreed merely that after twenty years Congress would be at liberty to abolish the slave-trade if it chose. By the same threat of disunion the Slave States of the extreme South gained other advantages. It was fixed by the

Constitution that a slave who fled to a Free State was not therefore to become a free man. He must be given back to his owner. It was yet further conceded that the Slave States should have increased political power in proportion to the number of their slaves. A black man did not count for so much as a white. Every State was to send members to the House of Representatives according to its population, and in reckoning that population five negroes were to be counted as three.

And yet at that time, and for years after, the opinion of the South itself regarded slavery as an evil—thrust upon them by England—difficult to be got rid of—profitable, it might be, but lamentable and temporary. No slave-holder refused to discuss the subject or admit the evils of the system. No violence was offered to those who denounced it. The clergy might venture to preach against it. Hopeful persons might foretell the approach of liberty to those unhappy captives. Even the lowest of the slave-holding class did not yet resent the expression of such hopes.

But a mighty change was destined to pass upon the tone of Southern opinion. The purchase of Louisiana opened a vast tract of the most fertile land in the world to the growth of cotton. Whitney's invention made the growth of cotton profitable. Slave-holding became lucrative. It was wealth to own a little plantation and a few negroes. There was an eager race for the possession of slaves. Importation alone could not supply the demand. Some of the more northerly of the Southern States turned their attention to the breeding of slaves for the Southern markets. Kentucky and Virginia became rich and infamous by this awful commerce.* While iniquity was not specially profitable, the Southern States were not very reluctant to be

---

* During the ten years, from 1840 to 1850, the annual export of slaves from the Border States to the South averaged 23,500. These, at an average value of £150, amounted to three millions and a quarter sterling!

virtuous. When the gains of wickedness became, as they now did, enormous, virtue ceased to have a footing in the South.

During many years the leader of the slave-owners was John C. Calhoun. He was a native of South Carolina—a tall, slender, gipsy-looking man, with an eye whose wondrous depth and power impressed all who came into his presence. Calhoun taught the people of the South that slavery was good for the slave. It was a benign, civilizing agency. The African attained to a measure of intelligence in slavery greatly in advance of that which he had ever reached as a free man. To him, visibly, it was a blessing to be enslaved. From all this it was easy to infer that Providence had appointed slavery for the advantage of both races; that opposition to this Heaven-ordained institution was profane; that abolition was merely an aspect of infidelity. So Calhoun taught. So the South learned to believe. Calhoun's last speech in Congress warned the North that opposition to slavery would destroy the Union. His latest conversation was on this absorbing theme. A few hours after, he had passed to where all dimness of vision is removed, and errors of judgment become impossible!

1850 A.D.

It was very pleasant for the slave-owners to be taught that slavery enjoyed divine sanction. The doctrine had other apostles than Mr. Calhoun. Unhappily it came to form part of the regular pulpit teaching of the Southern churches. It was gravely argued out from the Old Testament that slavery was the proper condition of the negro. Ham was to be the servant of his brethren. Hence all the descendants of Ham were the rightful property of white men. The slave who fled from his master was guilty of the crime of theft in one of its most heinous forms. So taught the Southern pulpit. Many books, written by grave divines for the enforcement of these doctrines, remain to awaken the amazement of posterity.

The slave-owners inclined a willing ear to these pleasing assurances. They knew slavery to be profitable. Their leaders in Church and State told them it was right. It was little wonder that a fanatical love to slavery possessed their hearts. In the passionate, ill-regulated minds of the slave-owning class it became in course of years almost a madness, which was shared, unhappily, by the great mass of the white population. Discussion could no longer be permitted. It became a fearful risk to express in the South an opinion hostile to slavery. It was a familiar boast that no man who opposed slavery would be suffered to live in a Slave State. And the slave-owners made their word good. Many suspected of hostile opinions were tarred and feathered and turned out of the State. Many were shot; many were hanged; some were burned. The Southern mobs were singularly brutal, and the slave-owners found willing hands to do their fiendish work. The law did not interfere to prevent or punish such atrocities. The churches looked on and held their peace.

As slave property increased in value, a strangely horrible system of laws gathered around it. The slave was regarded, not as a person, but as a thing. He had no civil rights; nay, it was declared by the highest legal authority that a slave had no rights at all which a white man was bound to respect. The most sacred laws of nature were defied. Marriage was a tie which bound the slave only during the master's pleasure. A slave had no more legal authority over his child "than a cow has over her calf." It was a grave offence to teach a slave to read. A white man might expiate that offence by fine or imprisonment; to a black man it involved flogging. The owner might not without challenge murder an unoffending slave; but a slave resisting his master's will might lawfully be slain. A slave who would not stand to be flogged, might be shot as he ran off. The master was blameless if his slave died under the administration of reasonable correction; in other words, if he flogged a slave to death. A fugitive slave might be killed by any means which his owner chose to employ. On the other hand, there was a slender pretext of laws for the protection of the slave. Any master, for instance, who wantonly cut out the tongue or put out the eyes of his slave, was liable to a small fine. But as no slave could give evidence affecting a white man in a court of law, the law had no terrors for the slave-owner.

The practice of the South in regard to her slaves was not unworthy of her laws. Children were habitually torn away from their mothers. Husbands and wives were habitually separated and forced to contract new marriages. Public whipping-houses became an institution. The hunting of escaped slaves became a regular profession. Dogs were bred and trained for that special work. Slaves who were suspected of an intention to escape were branded with red-hot irons. When the Northern armies forced their way into the South, many of the slaves who fled to them were found to be scarred or mutilated. The burning of a negro who was accused of crime was a familiar occurrence. It was a debated question whether it was more profitable to work the slaves moderately, and so make them last, or to take the greatest possible amount of work from them, even although that would quickly destroy them. Some favoured the plan of overworking, and acted upon it without scruple.

These things were done, and the Christian churches of the South were not ashamed to say that the system out of which they flowed enjoyed the sanction of God! It appeared that men who had spent their lives in the South were themselves so brutalized by their familiarity with the atrocities of slavery, that the standard by which they judged it was no higher than that of the lowest savages.

III.

MISSOURI.

When the State of Louisiana was received into the Union in 1812, there was left out a large proportion of the original purchase from Napoleon. As yet this region was unpeopled. It lay silent and unprofitable—a vast reserve prepared for the wants of unborn generations. It was traversed by the Missouri river. The great Mississippi was its boundary on the east. It possessed, in all, a navigable river-line of two thousand miles. Enormous mineral wealth was treasured up to enrich the world for centuries to come. There were coal-fields greater than those of all Europe. There was iron piled up in mountains, one of which contained two hundred millions of tons of ore. There was profusion of copper, of zinc, of lead. There were boundless forests. There was a soil unsurpassed in fertility. The climate was kindly and genial, marred by neither the stern winters of the North nor the fierce heats of the South. The scenery was often of rare beauty and grandeur.

This was the Territory of Missouri. Gradually settlers from the neighbouring States dropped in. Slave-holders came, bringing their chattels with them. They were first in the field, and they took secure possession. The free emigrant turned aside, and the slave-power reigned supreme in Missouri. The wealth and beauty of this glorious land were wedded to the most gigantic system of evil which ever established itself upon the Earth.

By the year 1818 there were sixty thousand persons residing

in Missouri. The time had come for the admission of this Territory into the Union as a State. It was the first great contest between the Free and the Slave States. The cotton-gin, the acquisition of Louisiana, the teaching of Calhoun, had done their work. The slave-owners were now a great political power—resolute, unscrupulous, intolerant of opposition. The next half century of American history takes its tone very much from their fierce and restless energy. Their policy never wavered. To gain predominance for slavery, with room for its indefinite expansion, these were their aims. American history is filled with their violence on to a certain April morning in 1865, when the slave-power and all its lawless pretensions lay crushed among the ruins of Richmond.

When the application of Missouri for admission into the Union came to be considered in Congress, an attempt was made to shut slavery wholly out of the new State. A struggle ensued which lasted for nearly three years. The question was one of vital importance. At this time the number of Free States and the number of Slave States were exactly equal. Whosoever gained Missouri gained a majority in the Senate. The North was deeply in earnest in desiring to prevent the extension of slavery. The South was equally resolute that no limitation should be imposed. The result was a compromise, proposed by the South. Missouri was to be given over to slavery. But it was agreed that, excepting within the limits of Missouri herself, slavery should not be permitted in any part of the territory purchased from France, north of a line drawn eastward and westward from the southern boundary of that State. Thus far might the waves of this foul tide flow, but no further. So ended the great controversy, in the decisive victory of the South.

IV.

HOPE FOR THE NEGRO.

The North participated in the gains of slavery. The cotton planter borrowed money at high interest from the Northern capitalist. He bought his goods in Northern markets. He sent his cotton to the North for sale. The Northern merchants made money at his hands, and were in no haste to overthrow the peculiar institution out of which results so pleasant flowed. They had no occasion, as the planter had, to persuade themselves that slavery enjoyed special divine sanction. But it did become a very general belief in the North that without slave-labour the cultivation of Southern lands was impossible. It was also very generally alleged that the condition of the slave was preferable to that of the free European labourer.

All looked very hopeless for the poor negro. The South claimed to hold him by divine right. She looked to a future of indefinite expansion. The boundless regions which stretched away from her border, untrodden by man, were marked out for slave territory. A powerful sentiment in the North supported her claims. She was able to exercise a controlling influence over the Federal Government. It seemed as if all authority in the Union was pledged to uphold slavery, and assert for ever the right of the white man to hold the black man as an article of merchandise.

But even then the awakening of the Northern conscience had begun. On the 1st of January 1831, a journeyman printer,

William Lloyd Garrison, published in Boston the first number of a paper devoted to the abolition of slavery. This is perhaps the earliest prominent incident in the history of Emancipation. It was indeed a humble opening of a noble career. Garrison was young and penniless. He wrote the articles; and he also, with the help of a friend, set the types. He lived mainly on bread and water. Only when a number of the paper sold particularly well, he and his companion indulged in a bowl of milk. The Mayor of Boston was asked by a Southern magistrate to suppress the paper. He replied that it was not worth the trouble. The office of the editor was "an obscure hole; his only visible auxiliary a negro boy; his supporters a few insignificant persons of all colours." The lordly Southerners need not be uneasy about this obscure editor and his paltry newspaper.

But the fulness of time had come, and every word spoken against slavery found now some willing listener. In the year after Garrison began his paper the American Anti-slavery Society was formed. It was composed of twelve members. Busy hands were scattering the seed abroad, and it sprang quickly. Within three years there were two hundred anti-slavery societies in America. In seven years more these had increased to two thousand. The war against slavery was now begun in earnest.

The slave-owners and their allies in the North regarded with rage unutterable this formidable invasion. Everywhere they opposed violence to the arguments of their opponents. Large rewards were offered for the capture of prominent abolitionists. Many Northern men, who unwarily strayed into Southern States, were murdered on the mere suspicion that they were opposed to slavery. President Jackson recommended Congress to forbid the conveyance to the South, by the mails, of anti-slavery publications. In Boston a mob of well-dressed and respectable citizens suppressed a meeting

1835
A.D.

of female abolitionists. While busied about that enterprise, they were fortunate enough to lay hold of Garrison, whose murder they designed, and would have accomplished, had not a timely sally of the constables rescued him from their grasp. In Connecticut a young woman was imprisoned for teaching negro children to read. Philadelphia was disgraced by riots in which negroes were killed and their houses burned down. Throughout the Northern States anti-slavery meetings were habitually invaded and broken up by the allies of the slave-owners. The abolitionists were devoured by a zeal which knew no bounds and permitted no rest. The slave-owners met them with a deep, remorseless, murderous hatred, which gradually possessed and corroded their whole nature. In this war, as it soon became evident, there could be no compromise. Peace was impossible otherwise than by the destruction of one or other of the contending parties. {1833 A.D.}

The spirit in which the South defended her cherished institution was fairly exemplified in her treatment of a young clergyman, Mr. Lovejoy, who offended her by his antipathy to slavery. Mr. Lovejoy established himself in Alton, a little town of Illinois, where he conducted a newspaper. Illinois was itself a Free State; but Missouri was near, and the slave-power was supreme in all that region. Mr. Lovejoy declared himself in his newspaper against slavery. He was requested to withdraw from that neighbourhood; but he maintained his right of free speech, and chose to remain. The mob sacked his printing-office, and flung his press into the river. Mr. Lovejoy bought another press. The arrival of this new machine highly displeased the ruffianism of the little town of Alton. It was stored for safety in a well-secured building, and two or three well-disposed citizens kept armed watch over it. The mob attacked the warehouse. Shots were exchanged, and some of the rioters were slain. At length the mob {1837 A.D.}

succeeded in setting fire to the building. When Mr. Lovejoy showed himself to the crowd he was fired at, and fell pierced by five bullets. The printing-press was broken; the newspaper was silenced; the hostile editor was slaughtered. The offended majesty of the slave-power was becomingly vindicated.

V.

TEXAS.

The decaying energies of Spain were sorely wasted by the wars which Napoleon forced upon her. Invaded, conquered, occupied, fought for during years by great armies, Spain issued from the struggle in a state of utter exhaustion. It was impossible that a country so enfeebled could maintain a great colonial dominion. Not long after the Battle of Waterloo all her American dependencies chose to be independent, and Spain could do nothing to prevent it. Among the rest, Mexico won for herself the privilege of self-government, of which she has thus far proved herself so incapable.

Lying between the Mississippi and the Rio Grande was a vast wilderness of undefined extent and uncertain ownership, which America, with some hesitation, recognized as belonging to Mexico. It was called Texas. The climate was genial; the soil was of wondrous fertility. America coveted this fair region, and offered to buy it from Mexico. Her offer was declined.

1829 A.D.

The great natural wealth of Texas, combined with the almost total absence of government, were powerful attractions to the lawless adventurers who abounded in the South-western States. A tide of vagrant blackguardism streamed into Texas. Safe from the grasp of justice, the murderer, the thief, the fraudulent debtor, opened in Texas a new and more hopeful career.

Founded by these conscript fathers, Texan society grew apace.

1836 A.D. In a few years Texas felt herself strong enough to be independent. Her connection with Mexico was declared to be at an end.

The leader in this revolution was Sam Houston, a Virginian of massive frame—energetic, audacious, unscrupulous—in no mean degree fitted to direct the storm he had helped to raise. For Houston was a Southerner, and it was his ambition to gain Texas for the purposes of the slave-owners. Mexico had abolished slavery. Texas could be no home for the possessor of slaves till she was severed from Mexico.

When independence was declared, Texas had to defend her newly-claimed liberties by the sword. General Houston

1836 A.D. headed the patriot forces, not quite 400 in number, and imperfectly armed. Santa Anna came against them with an army of 5000. The Texans retreated, and having nothing to carry, easily distanced their pursuers. At the San Jacinto, Houston was strengthened by the arrival of two field-pieces. He turned like a lion upon the unexpectant Mexicans, whom he caught in the very act of crossing the river. He fired grape-shot into their quaking ranks. His unconquerable Texans clubbed their muskets—they had no bayonets—and rushed upon the foe. The Mexicans fled in helpless rout, and Texas was free. The grateful Texans elected General Houston President of the republic which he had thus saved.

No sooner was Texas independent than she offered to join herself to the United States. Her proposals were at

1837 A.D. first declined. But the South warmly espoused her cause and urged her claims. Once more North and South met in fiery debate. Slavery had already a sure footing in Texas. If Texas entered the Union it was as a Slave State. On that ground avowedly the South urged the annexation. On that ground the North resisted it. "We all see," said Daniel Webster, "that Texas will be a slave-holding country; and I frankly avow my unwillingness to do anything which shall extend the slavery of the African race on this continent, or add another Slave-holding State to the Union." "The South," said the Legislature of Mississippi, speaking of slavery, "does not possess a blessing with which the affections of her people are so closely entwined, and whose value is more highly appreciated. By the annexation of Texas an equipoise of influence in the halls of Congress will be secured, which will furnish us a permanent guarantee of protection."

It was the battle-ground on which all the recent great battles of American political history have been fought. It ended, as such battles at that time usually did, in Southern victory. In March 1845 Texas was received into the Union. The slave-power gained new votes in Congress, and room for a vast extension of the slave-system.

VI.

THE WAR WITH MEXICO.

Mexico was displeased with the annexation of Texas, but did not manifest so quickly as it was hoped she would any disposition to avenge herself. Mr. Polk, a Southern man, was now President, and he governed in the interest of the South. A war with Mexico was a thing to be desired, because Mexico must be beaten, and could then be plundered of territory which the slave-owners would appropriate. To provoke Mexico the Unready, an army of 4000 men was sent to the extreme south-western confine of Texas. A Mexican army of 6000 lay near. The Americans, with marvellous audacity, erected a fort within easy range of Matamoras, a city of the Mexicans, and thus the city was in their power. After much hesitation the Mexican army attacked the Americans, and received, as they might well have anticipated, a severe defeat. Thus, without the formality of any declaration, the war was begun.

1846 A.D.

President Polk hastened to announce to Congress that the Mexicans had "invaded our territory, and shed the blood of our fellow-citizens." Congress voted men and money for the prosecution of the war. Volunteers offered themselves in multitudes. Their brave little army was in peril—far from help, and surrounded by enemies. The people were eager to support the heroes of whose victory they were so proud. And yet opinion was much divided. Many deemed the war unjust and disgraceful. Among these was a young lawyer of Illinois, destined in later years to fill a place in the hearts of his countrymen second only to that of Washington. Abraham Lincoln entered Congress while the war was in progress, and his first speech was in condemnation of the course pursued by the Government.

The war was pushed with vigour at first under the command of General Taylor, who was to become the next President; and finally under General Scott, who as a very young man had fought against the British at Niagara, and as a very old man was Commander-in-Chief of the American Army when the great war between North and South began. Many officers were there whose names became famous in after years. General Lee and General Grant gained here their first experience of war. They were not then known to each other. They met for the first time, twenty years after, in a Virginian cottage, to arrange terms of surrender for the defeated army of the Southern Confederacy!

The Americans resolved to fight their way to the enemy's capital, and there compel such a peace as would be agreeable to themselves. The task was not without difficulty. The Mexican army was greatly more numerous. They had a splendid cavalry force and an efficient artillery. Their commander, Santa Anna, unscrupulous even for a Mexican, was yet a soldier of some ability. The Americans were mainly volunteers who had never seen war till now. The fighting was severe. At Buena-Vista the American army was attacked by a force which outnumbered it in the proportion of five to one. The battle lasted for ten hours, and the invaders were saved from ruin by their superior artillery. The mountain passes were strongly fortified, and General Scott had to convey his army across chasms and ravines which the Mexicans, deeming them impracticable, had neglected to defend. Strong in the consciousness of their superiority to the people they invaded—the same consciousness which supported Cortes and his Spaniards three centuries before—the Americans pressed on. At length they came in sight of Mexico, at the same spot whence Cortes had viewed it. Once more they routed a Mexican army of greatly superior force, and then General Scott marched his little army of 6000 men quietly into the capital. The war was closed, and a treaty of peace was with little delay negotiated.

Sept. 14,
1847
A.D.

VII.

CALIFORNIA.

America exacted mercilessly the penalty which usually attends defeat. Mexico was to receive fifteen millions of dollars; but she ceded an enormous territory stretching westward from Texas to the Pacific.

One of the provinces which composed this magnificent prize was California. The slave-owners had gone to war with Mexico that they might gain territory which slavery should possess for ever. They sought to introduce California into the Union as a Slave State. But Providence interposed to shield her from a destiny so unhappy.

Just about the time that California became an American possession it was discovered that her soil was richly endowed with gold. On one of the tributaries of the Sacramento river an old settler was peacefully digging a trench—caring little, it may be supposed, about the change of citizenship which he had undergone—not dreaming that the next stroke of his spade was to influence the history not merely of California but of the world. Among the sand which he lifted were certain shining particles. His wondering eye considered them with attention. They were Gold! Gold was everywhere—in the soil, in the river-sand, in the mountain-rock; gold in dust, gold in pellets, gold in lumps! It was the land of old fairy tale, where wealth could be had by him who chose to stoop down and gather!

1848
A.D.

Fast as the mails could carry it the bewildering news thrilled the heart of America. To the energetic youth of the Northern States the charm was irresistible. It was now, indeed, a reproach to be poor, when it was so easy to be rich.

The journey to the land of promise was full of toil and danger. There were over two thousand miles of unexplored wilderness to traverse. There were mountain ranges to surmount, lofty and rugged as the Alps themselves. There were great desolate plains, unwatered and without vegetation. Indians, whose dispositions there was reason to question, beset the path. But danger was unconsidered. That season thirty thousand Americans crossed the plains, climbed the mountains, forded the streams, bore without shrinking all that want, exposure, and fatigue could inflict. Cholera broke out among them, and four thousand left their bones in the wilderness. The rest plodded on undismayed. Fifty thousand came by sea. From all countries they came—from quiet English villages, from the crowded cities of China. Before the year was out California had gained an addition of eighty thousand to her population.

These came mainly from the Northern States. They had no thought of suffering in their new home the evil institution of the South. They settled easily the constitution of their State, and California was received into the Union free from the taint of slavery.

1850 A.D.

It was no slight disappointment to the men of the South. They had urged on the war with Mexico in order to gain new Slave States, new votes in Congress, additional room for the spread of slavery. They had gained all the territory they hoped for, but this strange revelation of gold had peopled it from the North, and slavery was shut out for ever. To soothe their irritation, Henry Clay proposed a very black concession, under the disgrace of which America suffered for years in the estimation of all Christian nations. The South was angry, and hinted even then at secession. The North was prosperous. Her merchants were growing rich. Her farmers were rapidly overspreading the country and subduing waste lands to the service of man. Every year saw vast accessions to her wealth. Her supreme desire was for quietness. In this frame of mind she assented to the passing of the Fugitive Slave Law. Heretofore it had been lawful for the slave-owner to reclaim his slave who had escaped into a Free State; but although lawful it was in practice almost impossible. Now the officers of the Government, and all good citizens, were commanded to give to the pursuer all needful help. In certain cases Government was to defray the expense of restoring the slave to the plantation from which he had fled. In any trial arising under this law, the evidence of the slave himself was not to be received. The oath of his pursuer was almost decisive against him. Hundreds of Southern ruffians hastened to take vile advantage of this shameful law. They searched out coloured men in the Free States, and swore that they were escaped slaves. In too many instances they were successful, and many free negroes as well as escaped slaves were borne back to the miseries of slavery. The North erred grievously in consenting to a measure so base. It is just, however, to say, that although Northern politicians upheld it as a wise and necessary compromise, the Northern people in their hearts abhorred it. The law was so unpopular that its execution was resisted in several Northern cities, and it quickly passed into disuse.

VIII.

KANSAS.

The great Louisiana purchase from Napoleon was not yet wholly portioned off into States. Westward and northward of Missouri was an enormous expanse of the richest land in the Union, having as yet few occupants more profitable than the Indians. Two great routes of travel—to the west and to the south-west—traversed it. The eager searcher for gold passed that way on his long walk to California. The Mormon looked with indifference on its luxuriant vegetation as he toiled on to his New Jerusalem by the Great Salt Lake. In the year 1853 it was proposed to organize this region into two Territories, under the names of Kansas and Nebraska. Here once more arose the old question—Shall the Territories be Slave or Free? The Missouri Compromise had settled that slavery should never come here. But the slave-owners were able to cancel this settlement. A law was enacted under which the inhabitants were left to choose between slavery and freedom. The vote of a majority would decide the destiny of these magnificent provinces.

1854 A.D.

And now both parties had to bestir themselves. The early inhabitants of the infant States were to fix for all time whether they would admit or exclude the slave-owner with his victims. Everything depended, therefore, on taking early possession.

The South was first in the field. Missouri was near, and her citizens led the way. Great slave-owners took possession of lands in Kansas, and loudly invited their brethren from other States to come at once, bringing their slaves with them. But their numbers were small, while the need was urgent. The South had no population to spare fitted for the work of colonizing. But she had in large numbers the class of "mean whites." In the mean white of the Southern States we are permitted to see how low it is possible for our Anglo-Saxon humanity to fall. The mean white is entirely without education. His house is a hovel of the very lowest description. Personally he walks in rags and filth. He cannot stoop to work, because slavery has rendered labour disreputable. He supports himself as savages do—by shooting, by fishing, by the plunder of his industrious neighbours' fields and folds. The negro, out of the unutterable degradation to which he has been subjected, looks with scorn upon the mean white.

The mean whites of Missouri were easily marshalled for a raid into Kansas. The time came when elections were to take place—when the great question of Slave or Free was to be answered. Gangs of armed ruffians were marched over from Missouri. Such a party—nearly a thousand strong, accompanied by two pieces of cannon—entered the little town of Lawrence on the morning of the election-day. The ballot-boxes were taken possession of, and the peaceful inhabitants were driven away. The invaders cast fictitious votes into the boxes, outnumbering ten or twenty times the lawful roll of voters. A legislature wholly in the interests of slavery was thus elected. In due time that body began to enact laws. No man whose opinions were opposed to slavery was to be an elector in Kansas. Any man who spoke or wrote against slavery was to suffer imprisonment with hard labour. Death was the penalty for aiding the escape of a slave. All this was done while the enemies of slavery were an actual majority of the inhabitants of Kansas!

1855 A.D.

And then the Border ruffians overran the country—working their own wicked will wherever they came. The outrages they committed read like the freaks of demons. A man betted that he would scalp an abolitionist. He rode out from the little town of Leavenworth in search of a victim. He met a gentleman driving in a gig, shot him, scalped him, rode back to town, showed his ghastly trophy, and received payment of his bet. Men were gathered up from their work in the fields, ranged in line, and ruthlessly shot to death, because they hated slavery. A lawyer who had protested against frauds at an election was tarred and feathered; thus attired he was put up to auction, and sold to the highest bidder. The town of Lawrence was attacked by eight hundred marauders, who plundered it to their content —bombarding with artillery houses which displeased them— burning and destroying in utter wantonness.

But during all this unhappy time the steady tide of Northern emigration into Kansas flowed on. From the very outset of the strife the North was resolute to win Kansas for freedom. She sought to do this by colonizing Kansas with men who hated slavery. Societies were formed to aid poor emigrants. In single families, in groups of fifty to a hundred persons, the settlers were promptly moved westward. Some of these merely obeyed the impulse which drives so many Americans to leave the settled States of the east and push out into the wilderness. Others went that their votes might prevent the spread of slavery. There was no small measure of patriotism in the movement. Men left their comfortable homes in the east and carried their families into a wilderness, to the natural miseries of which was added the presence of bitter enemies. They did so that Kansas might be a Free State. Cannon were planted on the banks of the Missouri to prevent their entrance into Kansas. Many of them were plundered and turned back. Often their houses were burned and their fields wasted. But they were a self-reliant people, to whom it was no hardship to be obliged to defend themselves. When need arose they banded themselves together and gave battle to the ruffians who troubled them. And all the while they were growing stronger by constant reinforcements from the east. There were building, and clearing, and ploughing, and sowing. In spite of Southern outrage Kansas was fast ripening into a free and orderly community. In a few years the party of freedom was able to carry the elections. A constitution was adopted by which slavery was excluded from Kansas. And at length, just when the great final struggle between slavery and freedom was commencing, Kansas was received as a Free State. Her admission raised the number of States in the Union to thirty-four.

1859 A.D.

1861 A.D.

IX.

THE UNDERGROUND RAILWAY.

The conflict deepened as years passed. The Abolitionists became more irrepressible, the Slave-holders more savage. There seemed no hope of the law becoming just. The American people have a deep reverence for law, but here it was overborne by their sense of injustice. The wicked law was habitually set at defiance. Plans were carefully framed for aiding the escape of slaves. It was whispered about among the negroes that at certain points they were sure to find friends, shelter, safe conveyance to Canada. Around every plantation there stretched dense jungles, swamps, pathless forests. The escaping slave fled to these gloomy solitudes. They hunted him with blood-hounds, and many a poor wretch was dragged back to groan under deeper brutalities than before. If happily undiscovered, he made his way to certain well-known stations, a chain of which passed him safely on to the protection of the British flag. This was the Underground Railway. Now and then its agents were discovered. In that miserable time it was a grave offence to help a slave to escape. The offender was doomed to heavy fine or long imprisonment. Some died in prison of the hardships they endured. But the Underground Railway never wanted agents. No sooner had the unjust law claimed its victim than another stepped into his place. During many years the average number of slaves freed by this agency was considerably over a thousand.

The slave-holders made it unsafe for Northerners of anti-slavery opinions to remain in the South. Acts of brutal violence—very frequently resulting in murder—became very common. During one year eight hundred persons were robbed, whipped, tarred and feathered, or murdered for suspected antipathy to slavery. The possession of an anti-slavery newspaper or book involved expulsion from the State; and the circulation of such works could scarcely be expiated by any punishment but death. In Virginia and Maryland it was gravely contemplated to drive the free negroes from their homes, or to sell them into slavery and devote the money thus obtained to the support of the common schools! Arkansas did actually expel her free negroes. The slave-holders were determined that nothing which could remind their victims of liberty should be suffered to remain.

1860
A.D.

It was well said by Mr. Seward that they greatly erred who deemed this collision accidental or ephemeral. It was "an irrepressible conflict between opposing and enduring forces." All attempts at compromise would be short-lived and vain.

1858
A.D.

The most influential advocate of the numerous compromises by which the strife was sought to be calmed, was Henry Clay of Kentucky. Clay was much loved for his genial dispositions, much honoured and trusted in for his commanding ability. For many years of the prolonged struggle he seemed to stand between North and South — wielding authority over both. Although Southern, he hated slavery, and the slave-holders had often to receive from his lips emphatic denunciations of their favourite system. But he hated the doctrines of the abolitionists too, and believed they were leading towards the dissolution of the Union. He desired gradual emancipation, and along with it the return of the negroes to Africa. His aim was to deliver his country from the taint of slavery; but he would effect that great revolution step by step, as the country could bear it. At every crisis he was ready with a compromise. His proposals soothed the angry passions which were aroused when Missouri sought admission into the Union. His, too, was that unhappy compromise, one feature of which was the Fugitive Slave Bill. If compromise could have averted strife, Henry Clay would have saved his country. But the conflict was irrepressible.

1850 A.D.

The slave-power grew very bold during the later years of its existence. The re-opening of the slave-trade became one of the questions of the day in the Southern States. The Governor of South Carolina expressly recommended this measure. Southern newspapers supported it. Southern ruffians actually accomplished it. Numerous cargoes of slaves were landed in the South in open defiance of law, and the outrage was unrebuked. Political conventions voted their approval of the traffic. Associations were formed to promote it. Agricultural societies offered prizes for the best specimens of newly imported live Africans. It was even proposed that a prize should be offered for the best sermon in favour of the slave-trade! Advertisements like this were frequent in Southern newspapers—" For sale, four hundred negroes, lately landed on the coast of Texas." It was possible to do such things then. A little later—in the days of Abraham Lincoln—a certain ruffianly Captain Gordon made the perilous experiment of bringing a cargo of slaves to New York. He was seized, and promptly hanged. There was no further attempt to revive the slave-trade. Thus appropriately was this hideous traffic closed.

1859 A.D.

X.

JOHN BROWN.

The hatred of the North to slavery was rapidly growing. In the eyes of some slavery was an enormous sin, fitted to bring the curse of God upon the land. To others it was a political evil—marring the unity and hindering the progress of the country. To very many, on the one ground or the other, it was becoming hateful. Politicians sought to delay by concessions the inevitable crisis. Simple men, guiding themselves by their conviction of the wickedness of slavery, were growing ever more vehement in their hatred of this evil thing.

John Brown was such a man. The blood of the Pilgrim Fathers flowed in his veins. The old Puritan spirit guided all his actions. From his boyhood he abhorred slavery. He was constrained by his duty to God and man to spend himself in this cause. There was no hope of advantage in it; no desire for fame; no thought at all for himself or for his children. He saw a huge wrong, and he could not help setting himself to resist it. He was no politician. He was powerless to influence the councils of the nation. But he had the old Puritan aptitude for battle. He went to Kansas with his sons to help in the fight for freedom; and while there was fighting to be done, John Brown was at the front. He was a leader among the free settlers, who felt his military superiority, and followed him with confidence in many a bloody skirmish. He retired habitually into deep solitudes to pray. He had morning and evening prayers, in which all his followers joined. He would allow no man of immoral character in his camp. He believed that God directed him in visions. He was God's servant, and not man's. The work given him to do might be bitter to the flesh, but since it was God's work he dared not shrink from it.

When the triumph of freedom was secured in Kansas, John Brown moved eastward to Virginia. He was now to devote himself in earnest to the overthrow of the accursed institution. The laws of his country sanctioned an enormous wickedness. He declared war against his country, in so far as the national support of slavery was concerned. He prepared a constitution and a semblance of government. He himself was the head of this singular organization. Associated with him were a Secretary of State, a Treasurer, and a Secretary of War. Slavery, he stated, was a barbarous and unjustifiable war, carried on by one section of the community against another. His new government was for the defence of those whom the laws of the country wrongfully left undefended. He was joined by a few enthusiasts like-minded with himself. He laid up store of arms. He and his friends hung about plantations, and aided the escape of slaves to Canada. Occasionally the horses and cattle of the slave-owner were laid under contribution to support the costs of the campaign. Brown meditated war upon a somewhat extensive scale, and only waited the reinforcements of which he was assured, that he might proclaim liberty to all the captives in his neighbourhood. But reason appeared for believing that his plans had been betrayed to the enemy, and Brown was hurried into measures which brought swift destruction upon himself and his followers.

Harper's Ferry was a town of five thousand inhabitants, nestling amid steep and rugged mountains, where the Shenandoah unites its waters with those of the Potomac. The National Armory was here, and an arsenal in which were laid up enormous stores of arms and ammunition. Brown resolved to seize the arsenal. It was his hope that the slaves would hasten to his standard when the news of his success went abroad. And he seems to have reckoned that he would become strong enough to make terms with the Government, or, at the worst, to secure the escape to Canada of his armed followers.

One Sunday evening in October he marched into Harper's Ferry with a little army of twenty-two men—black and white—and easily possessed himself of the arsenal. He cut the telegraph wires. He stopped the trains which here cross the Potomac. He made prisoners of the workmen who came in the morning to resume their labours at the arsenal. His sentinels held the streets and bridges. The surprise was complete, and for a few hours his possession of the Government works was undisputed. **1859** A.D.

When at length the news of this amazing rebellion was suffered to escape, and America learned that old John Brown had invaded and conquered Harper's Ferry, the rage and alarm of the slave-owners and their supporters knew no bounds. The Virginians, upon whom the affront fell most heavily, took prompt measures to avenge it. By noon on Monday a force of militiamen surrounded the little town, to prevent the escape of those whom, as yet, they were not strong enough to capture. Before night fifteen hundred men were assembled. All that night Brown held his conquest. Nearly all his men were wounded or slain. His two sons were shot dead. Brown, standing beside their bodies, calmly exhorted his men to be firm, and sell their lives as dearly as possible. On Tuesday morning the soldiers forced an entrance, and Brown, with a sabre-cut in his head, and two bayonet-stabs in his body, was a prisoner. He was tried and condemned to die. Throughout his imprisonment, and even amid the horrors of the closing scene, his habitual serenity was undisturbed. He "humbly trusted that he had the peace of God, which passeth all understanding, to rule in his heart."

To the enraged slave-owners John Brown was a detestable rebel. To the abolitionists he was a martyr. To us he is a true, earnest, but most ill-judging man. His actions were unwise, unwarrantable; but his aims were noble, his self-devotion was heroic.

XI.

EIGHTEEN HUNDRED AND SIXTY.

In this year America made her decennial enumeration of her people and their possessions. The industrial greatness which the census revealed was an astonishment not only to the rest of the world, but even to herself. The slow growth of the old European countries seemed absolute stagnation beside this swift multiplication of men and of beasts, and of wealth in every form.

The three millions of colonists who had thrown off the British yoke had now increased to thirty-one and a half millions! Of these, four millions were slaves, owned by three hundred and fifty thousand persons. This great population was assisted in its toils by six millions of horses and two millions of working oxen. It owned eight millions of cows, fifteen millions of other cattle, twenty-two millions of sheep, and thirty-three millions of hogs. The products of the soil were enormous. The cotton crop of that year was close upon one million tons. It had more than doubled within the last ten years. The grain crop was twelve hundred millions of bushels—figures so large as to pass beyond our comprehension. Tobacco had more than doubled since 1850—until now America actually yielded a supply of five hundred millions of pounds. There were five thousand miles of canals, and thirty thousand miles of railroad—twenty-two thousand of which were the creation of the preceding ten years. The textile manufactures of the country had reached the annual value of forty millions sterling. America had provided for the education of her children by erecting one hundred and thirteen thousand schools and colleges, and employing one hundred and fifty thousand teachers. Her educational institutions enjoyed revenues amounting to nearly seven millions sterling, and were attended by five millions and a half of pupils. Religious instruction was given in fifty-four thousand churches, in which there was accommodation for nineteen millions of hearers. The daily history of the world was supplied by four thousand newspapers, which circulated annually one thousand millions of copies.

There belonged to the American people nearly two thousand millions of acres of land. They had not been able to make any use of the greater part of this enormous heritage. Only four hundred millions of acres had as yet become in any measure available for the benefit of man. The huge remainder lay unpossessed—its power to give wealth to man growing always greater during the long ages of solitude and neglect. The ownership of this prodigious expanse of fertile land opened to the American people a future of unexampled prosperity. They needed only peace and the exercise of their own vigorous industry. But a sterner task was in store for them.

During the last few years the divisions between North and South had become exceedingly bitter. The North was becoming ever more intolerant of slavery. The unreasoning and passionate South resented with growing fierceness the Northern abhorrence of her favoured institution. In the Senate House one day a member was bending over his desk busied in writing. His name was Charles Sumner, of Massachusetts. He was well known for the hatred which he bore to slavery, and his power as an orator gave him rank as a leader among those who desired the overthrow of the system. While this senator was occupied with his writing, there walked up to him two men whom South Carolina deemed not unworthy to frame laws for a great people. One of them—a ruffian, although a senator—whose name was Brooks, carried a heavy cane. With this formidable weapon he discharged many blows upon the head of the unsuspecting Sumner, till his victim fell bleeding and senseless to the floor. For this outrage a trifling fine was imposed on Brooks. His admiring constituents eagerly paid the amount. Brooks resigned his seat. He was immediately re-elected. Handsome canes flowed in upon him from all parts of the slave country. The South, in a most deliberate and emphatic manner, recorded its approval of the crime which he had committed.

To such a pass had North and South now come. Sumner vehemently attacking slavery; Brooks vehemently smiting Sumner upon his defenceless head—these men represent with perfect truthfulness the feeling of the two great sections. This cannot last.

A new President fell to be elected in 1860. Never had an election taken place under circumstances so exciting. The North was thoroughly aroused on the slave question. The time for compromises was felt to have passed. It was a death-grapple between the two powers. Peaceful arrangement was hopeless. Each party had to put forth its strength and conquer or be crushed.

The enemies of slavery announced it as their design to prevent slavery from extending to the Territories. They had no power to interfere in States where the system already exists. But the Territories belong to the Union. The proper condition of the Union is freedom. The Slave States are merely exceptional. It is contrary to the Constitution to carry this irregularity where it does not already exist.

The Territories, said the South, belong to the Union. All citizens of the Union are free to go there with their property.

Slaves are property. Slavery may therefore be established in the Territories if slave-owners choose to settle there.

On this issue battle was joined. The Northern party nominated Abraham Lincoln as their candidate. The Southerners, with their friends in the North—of whom there were many—divided their votes among three candidates. They were defeated, and Abraham Lincoln became President.

Mr. Lincoln was the son of a small and not very prosperous farmer. He was born in 1809 in the State of Kentucky; but his youth was passed mainly in Indiana. His father had chosen to settle on the furthest verge of civilization. Around him was a dense illimitable forest, still wandered over by the Indians. Here and there in the wilderness occurred a rude wooden hut like his own, the abode of some rough settler—regardless of comfort and greedy of the excitements of pioneering. The next neighbour was two miles away. There were no roads, no bridges, no inns. The traveller swam the rivers he had to cross, and trusted, not in vain, to the hospitality of the settlers for food and shelter. Now and then a clergyman passed that way, and from a hasty platform beneath a tree the gospel was preached to an eagerly-listening audience of rugged woodsmen. Many years after, when he had grown wise and famous, Mr. Lincoln spoke, with tears in his eyes, of a well-remembered sermon which he had heard from a wayfaring preacher in the great Indiana wilderness. Justice was administered under the shade of forest trees. The jury sat upon a log. The same tree which sheltered the court, occasionally served as a gibbet for the criminal.

In this society—rugged, but honest and kindly—the youth of the future President was passed. He had little schooling. Indeed there was scarcely a school within reach, and if all the days of his school-time were added together they would scarcely make up one year. His father was poor, and Abraham was needed on the farm. There was timber to fell, there were fences to build, fields to plough, sowing and reaping to be done. Abraham led a busy life, and knew well, while yet a boy, what hard work meant. Like all boys who come to anything great, he had a devouring thirst for knowledge. He borrowed all the books in his neighbourhood, and read them by the blaze of the logs which his own axe had split.

This was his upbringing. When he entered life for himself it was as clerk in a small store. He served nearly a year there, conducting faithfully and cheerfully the lowly commerce by which the wants of the settlers were supplied. Then he comes before us as a soldier, fighting a not very bloody campaign against the Indians, who had undertaken, rather imprudently, to drive the white men out of that region. Having settled in Illinois, he commenced the study of law, supporting himself by land-surveying during the unprofitable stages of that pursuit. Finally he applied himself to politics, and in 1834 was elected a member of the Legislature of Illinois.

He was now in his twenty-fifth year; of vast stature, somewhat awkwardly fashioned, slender for his height, but uncommonly muscular and enduring. He was of pleasant humour, ready and true insight. After such a boyhood as his, difficulty had no terrors for him, and he was incapable of defeat. His manners were very homely. His lank, ungainly figure, dressed in the native manufacture of the backwoods, would have spread dismay in a European drawing-room. He was smiled at even in the uncourtly Legislature of Illinois. But here, as elsewhere, whoever came into contact with Abraham Lincoln felt that he was a man framed to lead other men. Sagacious, penetrating, full of resource, and withal honest, kindly, conciliatory, his hands might be roughened by toil, his dress and ways might be those of the wilderness, yet was he quickly recognized as a born King of men.

During the next twenty-six years Mr. Lincoln applied himself to the profession of the law. During the greater portion of those years he was in public life. He had part in all the political controversies of his time. Chief among these were the troubles arising out of slavery. From his boyhood Mr. Lincoln was a steady enemy to slavery, as at once foolish and wrong. He would not interfere with it in the old States, for there the Constitution gave him no power; but he would in no ways allow its establishment in the Territories. He desired a policy which "looked forward hopefully to the time when slavery, as a wrong, might come to an end." He gained in a very unusual degree the confidence of his party, who raised him to the presidential chair, as a true and capable representative of their principles in regard to the great slavery question.

XII.

SECESSION.

South Carolina was the least loyal to the Union of all the States. She estimated very highly her own dignity as a sovereign State. She held in small account the allegiance which she owed to the Federal Government. Twenty-eight years ago Congress had enacted a highly protective tariff. South Carolina, disapproving of this measure, decreed that it was not binding upon her. Should the Federal Government attempt to enforce it, South Carolina announced her purpose of quitting the Union and becoming independent. General Jackson, who was then President, made ready to hold South Carolina to her duty by force; but Congress modified the tariff, and so averted the danger. Jackson believed firmly that the men who then held the destiny of South Carolina in their hands wished to secede. "The tariff," he said, "was but a pretext. The next will be the slavery question."

1832 A.D.

The time predicted had now come, and South Carolina led her sister States into the dark and bloody path. A convention of her people was promptly called, and on the 20th of December an Ordinance was passed dissolving the Union, and declaring South Carolina a free and independent republic. When the Ordinance was passed the bells of Charleston rang for joy, and the streets of the city resounded with the wild exulting shouts of an excited people. Dearly had the joy of those tumultuous hours to be paid for. Four years later, when

1860 A.D.

Sherman quelled the heroic defence of the rebel city, Charleston lay in ruins. Her people, sorely diminished by war and famine, had been long familiar with the miseries which a strict blockade and a merciless bombardment can inflict.

The example of South Carolina was at once followed by other discontented States. Georgia, Alabama, Mississippi, Louisiana, and Florida hastened to assert their independence, and to league themselves into a new Confederacy. They adopted a Constitution, differing from the old mainly in these respects, that it contained provisions against taxes to protect any branch of industry, and gave effective securities for the permanence and extension of slavery. They elected Mr. Jefferson Davis President for six years. They possessed themselves of the Government property within their own boundaries. It was not yet their opinion that the North would fight, and they bore themselves with a high hand in all the arrangements which their new position seemed to call for.

After the Government was formed, the Confederacy was joined by other Slave States who at first had hesitated. Virginia, North Carolina, Tennessee, Arkansas, and Texas, after some delay gave in their adhesion. The Confederacy in its completed form was composed of eleven States, with a population of nine millions; six millions of whom were free, and three millions were slaves. Twenty-three States remained loyal to the Union. Their population amounted to twenty-two millions.

It is not to be supposed that the free population of the seceding States were unanimous in their desire to break up the Union. On the contrary, there is good reason to believe that a majority of the people in most of the seceding States were all the time opposed to secession. In North Carolina the attempt to carry secession was at first defeated by the people. In the end that State left the Union reluctantly, under the belief that not otherwise could it escape becoming the battle-ground of the contending powers. Thus, too, Virginia refused at first by large majorities to secede. In Georgia and Alabama the minorities against secession were large. In Louisiana 20,000 votes were given for secession, and 17,000 against it. In many cases it required much intrigue and dexterity of management to obtain a favourable vote; and the resolution to quit the Union was received in sorrow by very many of the Southern people. But everywhere in the South the idea prevailed that allegiance was due to the State rather than to the Federation. And thus it came to pass that when the authorities of a State resolved to abandon the Union, the citizens of that State felt constrained to secede even while they mourned the course upon which they were forced to enter.

It has been maintained by some defenders of the seceding States that slavery was not the cause of secession. On that question there can surely be no authority so good as that of the seceding States themselves. A declaration of the reasons which influenced their action was issued by several States, and acquiesced in by the others. South Carolina was the first to give reasons for her conduct. These reasons related wholly to slavery. No other cause of separation was hinted at. The Northern States, it was complained, would not restore runaway slaves. They assumed the right of "deciding on the propriety of our domestic institutions." They denounced slavery as sinful. They permitted the open establishment of anti-slavery societies. They aided the escape of slaves. They sought to exclude slavery from the Territories. Finally, they had elected to the office of President Abraham Lincoln, "a man whose opinions and purposes are hostile to slavery."

Some of the American people had from the beginning held the opinion that any State could leave the Union at her pleasure. That belief was general in the South. The seceding States did not doubt that they had full legal right to take the step which they had taken. And they stated with perfect frankness what was their reason for exercising this right. They believed that slavery was endangered by their continuance in the Union. Strictly speaking, they fought in defence of their right to secede. But they had no other motive for seceding than that slavery should be preserved and extended. The war which ensued was therefore really a war in defence of slavery. But for the Southern love and the Northern antipathy to slavery, no war could have occurred. The men of the South attempted to break up the Union because they thought slavery would be safer if the Slave-owning States stood alone. The men of the North refused to allow the Union to be broken up. They did not go to war to put down slavery. They had no more right to put down slavery in the South than England has to put down slavery in Cuba. The Union which they loved was endangered, and they fought to defend the Union.

XIII.

THE TWO PRESIDENTS.

Mr. Lincoln was elected, according to usage, early in November, but did not take possession of his office till March. In the interval President Buchanan remained in power. This gentleman was Southern by birth, and, as it has always been believed, by sympathy. He laid no arrest upon the movements of the seceding States; nay, it has been alleged that he rather sought to remove obstacles from their path. During all these winter months the Southern leaders were suffered to push forward their preparations for the approaching conflict. The North still hoped for peace. Congress busied itself with vain schemes of conciliation. Meetings were held all over the country, at which an anxious desire was expressed to remove causes of offence. The self-willed Southerners would listen to no compromise. They would go apart, peacefully if they might; in storm and bloodshed if they must.

Early in February Mr. Lincoln left his home in Illinois on his way to Washington. His neighbours accompanied him to the railroad depôt, where he spoke a few parting words to them. "I know not," he said, "how soon I shall see you again. A duty devolves upon me, which is, perhaps, greater than that which has devolved upon any other man since the days of Washington. He never would have succeeded except for the aid of Divine Providence, upon which he at all times relied. I feel that I cannot succeed with-

1861
A.D.

out the same divine aid which sustained him, and on the same Almighty Being I place my reliance for support; and I hope you, my friends, will all pray that I may receive that divine assistance without which I cannot succeed, but with which success is certain."

With these grave, devout words, he took his leave, and passed on to the fulfilment of his heavy task. His inauguration took place as usual on the 4th of March. A huge crowd assembled around the Capitol. Mr. Lincoln had thus far kept silence as to the course he meditated in regard to the seceding States. Seldom had a revelation involving issues so momentous been waited for at the lips of any man. The anxious crowd stood so still, that to its utmost verge the words of the speaker were distinctly heard.

He assured the Southerners that their fears were unfounded. He had no lawful right to interfere with slavery in the States where it exists; he had no purpose and no inclination to interfere. He would, on the contrary, maintain them in the enjoyment of all the rights which the Constitution bestowed upon them. But he held that no State could quit the Union at pleasure. In view of the Constitution and the laws, the Union was unbroken. His policy would be framed upon that belief. He would continue to execute the laws within the seceding States, and would continue to possess Federal property there, with all the force at his command. That did not necessarily involve conflict or bloodshed. Government would not assail the discontented States, but would suffer no invasion of its constitutional rights. With the South, therefore, it lay to decide whether there was to be peace or war.

A week or two before Mr. Lincoln's inauguration Jefferson Davis had entered upon his career as President of the Southern Republic. Mr. Davis was an old politician. He had long advocated the right of an aggrieved State to leave the Union; and he had largely contributed, by speech and by intrigue, to hasten the crisis which had now arrived. He was an accomplished man, a graceful writer, a fluent and persuasive speaker. He was ambitious, resolute, and of ample experience in the management of affairs; but he had many disqualifications for high office. His obstinacy was blind and unreasoning. He had little knowledge of men, and could not distinguish "between an instrument and an obstacle." His moral tone was low. He taught Mississippi, his native State, to repudiate her just debts. A great English statesman, who made his acquaintance some years before the war broke out, pronounced him one of the ablest and one of the most wicked men in America.

In his Inaugural Address Mr. Davis displayed a prudent reserve. Speaking for the world to hear—a world which, upon the whole, abhorred slavery—he did not name the grievances which rendered secession necessary. He maintained the right of a discontented State to secede. The Union had ceased to answer the ends for which it was established; and in the exercise of an undoubted right they had withdrawn from it. He hoped their late associates would not incur the fearful responsibility of disturbing them in their pursuit of a separate political career. If so, it only remained for them to appeal to arms, and invoke the blessing of Providence on a just cause.

Alexander H. Stephens was the Vice-President of the Confederacy. His health was bad, and the expression of his face indicated habitual suffering. He had nevertheless been a laborious student, and a patient, if not a very wise, thinker on the great questions of his time. In the early days of secession he delivered at Savannah a speech which quickly became famous, and which retains its interest still as the most candid explanation of the motives and the expectations of the South. The old Government, he said, was founded upon sand. It was founded upon the assumption of the equality of races. Its authors entertained the mistaken belief that African slavery was wrong in principle. "Our new Government," said the Vice-President, "is founded upon exactly the opposite ideas; its foundations are laid, its corner-stone rests, upon the great truth that the negro is not equal to the white man; that slavery is his natural and normal condition." Why the Creator had made him so could not be told. "It is not for us to inquire into the wisdom of His ordinances, or to question them." With this very clear statement by the Vice-President, we are freed from uncertainty as to the designs of the Southern leaders, and filled with thankfulness for the ruin which fell upon their wicked enterprise.

It is a very curious but perfectly authenticated fact, that notwithstanding the pains taken by Southern leaders to show that they seceded merely to preserve and maintain slavery, there were many intelligent men in England who steadfastly maintained that slavery had little or nothing to do with the origin of the Great War.

BOOK IV.

I.

THE FIRST BLOW STRUCK.

When his Inaugural Address was delivered, Mr. Lincoln was escorted by his predecessor in office back to the White House, where they parted—Buchanan to retire, not with honour, into a kindly oblivion; Lincoln to begin that great work which had devolved upon him. During all that month of March and on to the middle of April the world heard very little of the new President. He was seldom seen in Washington. It was rumoured that intense meditation upon the great problem had made him ill. It was asserted that he endured the pains of indecision. In the Senate attempts were made to draw forth from him a confession of his purposes—if indeed he had any purposes. But the grim silence was unbroken. The South persuaded herself that he was afraid—that the peace-loving, money-making North had no heart for fight. She was even able to believe, in her vain pride, that most of the Northern States would ultimately adopt her doctrines and join themselves to her Government. Even in the North there was a party which wished union with the seceding States, on their own principles. There was a general indisposition to believe in war. The South had so often threatened, and been so often soothed by fresh concessions, it was difficult to believe now that she meant anything more than to establish a position for advantageous negotiation. All over the world men waited in anxious suspense for the revelation of President Lincoln's policy. Mercantile enterprise languished. Till the occupant of the White House chose to open his lips and say whether it was peace or war, the business of the world must be content to stand still.

Mr. Lincoln's silence was not the result of irresolution. He had doubt as to what the South would do. He had no doubt as to what he himself would do. He would maintain the Union;— by friendly arrangement and concession, if that were possible; if not, by war fought out to the bitter end.

He nominated the members of his Cabinet—most prominent among whom was William H. Seward, his Secretary of State. Mr. Seward had been during all his public life a determined enemy to slavery. He was in full sympathy with the President as to the course which had to be pursued. His acute and vigorous intellect and great experience in public affairs fitted him for the high duties which he was called to discharge.

So soon as Mr. Lincoln entered upon his office the Southern Government sent ambassadors to him as to a foreign power. These gentlemen formally intimated that the six States had withdrawn from the Union, and now formed an independent nation. They desired to solve peaceably all the questions growing out of this separation, and they desired an interview with the President, that they might enter upon the business to which they had been appointed.

Mr. Seward replied to the communication of the Southern envoys. His letter was framed with much care, as its high importance demanded. It was calm and gentle in its tone, but most clear and decisive. He could not recognize the events which had recently occurred as a rightful and accomplished revolution, but rather as a series of unjustifiable agressions.

He could not recognize the new Government as a government at all. He could not recognize or hold official intercourse with its agents. The President could not receive them or admit them to any communication. Within the unimpassioned words of Mr. Seward there breathed the fixed, unalterable purpose of the Northern people, against which, as many persons even then felt, the impetuous South might indeed dash herself to pieces, but could by no possibility prevail. The baffled ambassadors went home, and the angry South quickened her preparations for war.

Within the bay of Charleston, and intended for the defence of that important city, stood Fort Sumpter, a work of considerable strength, and capable, if adequately garrisoned, of a prolonged defence. It was not so garrisoned, however, when the troubles began. It was held by Major Anderson with a force of seventy men, imperfectly provisioned. The Confederates wished to possess themselves of Fort Sumpter, and hoped at one time to effect their object peaceably. When that hope failed them, they cut off Major Anderson's supply of provisions, and quietly began to encircle him with batteries. For some time they waited till hunger should compel the surrender of the fort. But word was brought to them that President Lincoln was sending ships with provisions. Fort Sumpter was promptly summoned to surrender. Major Anderson offered to go in three days, if not relieved. In reply he received intimation that in one hour the bombardment would open.   April 11, **1861** A.D.

About daybreak on the 12th the stillness of Charleston bay was disturbed by the firing of a large mortar and the shriek of a shell as it rushed through the air. The shell burst over Fort Sumpter, and the war of the Great Rebellion was begun. The other batteries by which the doomed fortress was surrounded quickly followed, and in a few minutes fifty guns of the largest size flung shot and shell into the works. The guns were admirably served, and every shot told. The garrison had neither provisions nor an adequate supply of ammunition. They were seventy, and their assailants were seven thousand. All they could do was to offer such resistance as honour demanded. Hope of success there was none.

The garrison did not reply at first to the hostile fire. They quietly breakfasted in the security of the bomb-proof casemates. Having finished their repast, they opened a comparatively feeble and ineffective fire. All that day and next the Confederate batteries rained shell and red-hot shot into the fort. The wooden barracks caught fire and the men were nearly suffocated by the smoke. Barrels of gunpowder had to be rolled through the flames into the sea. The last cartridge had been loaded into the guns. The last biscuit had been eaten. Huge clefts yawned in the crumbling walls. Enough had been done for honour. To prolong the resistance was uselessly to endanger the lives of brave men. Major Anderson surrendered the ruined fortress, and marched out with the honours of war. Curiously enough, although heavy firing had continued during thirty-four hours, no man on either side was injured!

It was a natural mistake that South Carolina should deem the capture of Fort Sumpter a glorious victory. The bells of Charleston chimed triumphantly all the day; guns were fired; the citizens were in the streets expressing with many oaths the rapture which this great success inspired, and their confident hope of triumphs equally decisive in time to come; ministers gave thanks; ladies waved handkerchiefs; male patriots quaffed potent draughts to the welfare of the Confederacy. On that bright April Sunday all was enthusiasm and boundless excitement in the city of Charleston. Alas for the vanity of human hopes! There were days near at hand, and many of them too, when these rejoicing citizens should sit in hunger and sorrow and despair among the ruins of their city and the utter wreck of their fortunes and their trade.

By many of the Southern people war was eagerly desired. The Confederacy was already established for some months, and yet it included only six States. There were eight other Slave States, whose sympathies it was believed were with the seceders. These had been expected to join, but there proved to exist within them a loyalty to the Union sufficiently strong to delay their secession. Amid the excitements which war would enkindle, this loyalty, it was hoped, would disappear, and the hesitating States would be constrained to join their fortunes to those of their more resolute sisters. The fall of Fort Sumpter was more than a military triumph. It would more than double the strength of the Confederacy and raise it at once to the rank of a great power. Everywhere in the South, therefore, there was a wild, exulting joy. And not without reason. Virginia, North Carolina, Tennessee, Arkansas, and Texas now joined their sisters in secession.

In the North, the hope had been tenaciously clung to that the peace of the country was not to be disturbed. This dream was rudely broken by the siege of Fort Sumpter. The North awakened suddenly to the awful certainty that civil war was begun. There was a deep feeling of indignation at the traitors who were willing to ruin their country that slavery might be secure. There was a full appreciation of the danger. There was an instant universal determination that, at whatever cost, the national life must be preserved. Personal sacrifice was unconsidered. Individual interests were merged in the general good. Political difference, ordinarily so bitter, was for the time almost effaced. Nothing was of interest but the question how this audacious rebellion was to be suppressed and the American nation upheld in the great place which it claimed among men.

Two days after the fall of Fort Sumpter, Mr. Lincoln intimated, by proclamation, the dishonour done to the laws of the United States, and called out the militia to the extent of 75,000 men. The Free States responded enthusiastically to the call. So prompt was their action, that on the very next day several companies arrived in Washington. Flushed by their easily-won victory, the Southerners talked boastfully of seizing the capital. In very short space there were 50,000 loyal men ready to prevent that, and the safety of Washington was secured.

The North pushed forward with boundless energy her warlike preparations. Rich men offered money with so much liberality that in a few days nearly five millions sterling had been contributed. The school-teachers of Boston dedicated fixed proportions of their incomes to the support of the Government, while the war should last. All over the country the excited people gathered themselves into crowded meetings, and breathed forth in fervid resolutions their determination to spend fortune and life in defence of the Union. Volunteer companies were rapidly formed. In the cities ladies began to organize themselves for the relief of sick and wounded soldiers. It had been fabled that the North would not fight. With a fiery promptitude unknown before in modern history the people sprang to arms.

Even yet there was on both sides a belief that the war would be a short one. The South, despising an adversary unpractised in war, and vainly trusting that the European powers would interfere in order to secure their wonted supplies of cotton, expected that a few victories more would bring peace. The North still regarded secession as little more than a gigantic riot, which she proposed to extinguish within ninety days. The truth was strangely different from the prevailing belief of the day. A high-spirited people, six millions in number, occupying a fertile territory nearly a million square miles in extent, had risen against the Government. The task undertaken by the North was to conquer this people, and by force of arms to bring them and their territory back to the Union. This was not likely to prove a work of easy accomplishment.

II.

THE BATTLE OF BULL RUN.

When the North addressed herself to her task, her own capital was still threatened by the rebels. Two or three miles down the Potomac, and full in view of Washington, lies the old-fashioned decaying Virginian town of Alexandria, where the unfortunate Braddock had landed his troops a century before. The Confederate flag floated over Alexandria. A rebel force was marching on Harper's Ferry, forty miles from Washington; and as the Government works there could not be defended, they were burned. Preparations were being made to seize Arlington Heights, from which Washington could be easily shelled. At Manassas Junction, thirty miles away, a rebel army lay encamped. It seemed to many foreign observers that the North might lay aside all thought of attack, and be well pleased if she succeeded in the defence of what was still left to her.

But the Northern people, never doubting either their right or their strength, put their hand boldly to the work. The first thing to be done was to shut the rebels in so that no help could reach them from the world outside. They could grow food enough, but they were a people who could make little. They needed from Europe supplies of arms and ammunition, of clothing, of medicine. They needed money, which they could only get by sending away their cotton. To stop their intercourse with Europe was to inflict a blow which would itself prove almost fatal. Four days after the fall of Fort Sumpter, Mr. Lincoln announced the blockade of all the rebel ports. It was a little time after till he had ships enough to make the blockade effective. But in a few weeks this was done, and every rebel port was closed. The grasp thus established was never relaxed. So long as the war lasted, the South obtained foreign supplies only from vessels which carried on the desperate trade of blockade-running.

Virginia completed her secession on the 23rd April. Next morning Federal troops seized and fortified Alexandria and the Arlington Heights. In the western portions of Virginia the people were so little in favour of secession that they wished to establish themselves as a separate State—loyal to the Union. With no very serious trouble the rebel forces were driven out of this region, and Western Virginia was restored to the Union. Desperate attempts were made by the disloyal Governor of Missouri to carry his State out of the Union, against the wish of a majority of the people. It was found possible to defeat the efforts of the secessionists and retain Missouri. Throughout the war this State was grievously wasted by Southern raids, but she held fast her loyalty.

Thus at the opening of the war substantial advantages had been gained by the North. They were not, however, of a sufficiently brilliant character fully to satisfy the expectations of the excited people. A great battle must be won. Government, unwisely yielding to the pressure, ordered their imperfectly disciplined troops to advance and attack the rebels in their position at Manassas Junction.

General Beauregard lay at Manassas with a rebel force variously estimated at from 30,000 to 40,000 men. In front of his position ran the little stream of Bull Run, in a narrow, wooded valley—the ground rising on either side into "bluffs," crowned with frequent patches of dense wood. General M'Dowell moved to attack him, with an army about equal in strength. It was early Sunday morning when the army set out from its quarters at Centreville. The march was not over ten miles, but the day was hot, and the men not yet inured to hardship. It was ten o'clock when the battle fairly opened. From the heights on the northern bank of the stream the Federal artillery played upon the enemy. The Southern line stretched well-nigh ten miles. M'Dowell hoped by striking with an overwhelming force at a point on the enemy's right, to roll back his entire line in confusion. Heavy masses of infantry forded the stream and began the attack. The Southerners fought bravely and skilfully, but at the point of attack they were inferior in number, and they were driven back. The battle spread away far among the woods, and soon every copse held its group of slain and wounded men. By three o'clock the Federals reckoned the battle as good as won. The enemy, though still fighting, was falling back. But at that hour a railway train ran close up to the field of battle with 15,000 Southerners fresh and eager for the fray. This new force was hurried into action. The wearied Federals could not endure the vehemence of the attack. They broke and fled down the hill-side. With inexperienced troops a measured and orderly retreat is impossible. Defeat is quickly followed by panic. The men who had fought so bravely all the day now hurried in wild confusion from the field. The road was choked with a tangled mass of baggage-waggons, artillery, soldiers and civilians frenzied by fear, and cavalry riding wildly through the quaking mob. But the Southerners attempted no pursuit, and the panic passed away. Scarcely an attempt, however, was made to stop the flight. Order was not restored till the worn-out men made their way back to Washington.

July 21, 1861 A.D.

This was the first great battle of the war, and its results were of prodigious importance. By the sanguine men of the South it was hailed as decisive of their final success. President Davis counted upon the immediate recognition of the Confederacy by the great powers of Europe as now certain. The newspapers accepted it as a settled truth that " one Southerner was equal to five Yankees." Intrigues began for the succession to the presidential chair—six years hence. A controversy arose among the States as to the location of the Capital. The success of the Confederacy was regarded as a thing beyond doubt. Enlistment languished. It was scarcely worth while to undergo the inconvenience of fighting for a cause which was already triumphant.

The defeat at Manassas taught the people of the North that the task they had undertaken was a heavier task than they supposed. But it did not shake their steady purpose to perform it. On the day after the battle—while the routed army was swarming into Washington—Congress voted five hundred millions of dollars, and called for half a million of volunteers. A few days later, Congress unanimously resolved that the suppression of the rebellion was a sacred duty, from the performance of which no disaster should discourage; to which they pledged the employment of every resource, national and individual. " Having chosen our course" said Mr. Lincoln, " without guile, and with pure purpose, let us renew our trust in God, and go forward without fear and with manly hearts." The spirit of the North rose as the greatness of the enterprise became apparent. No thought was there of any other issue from the national agony than the overthrow of the national foe. The youth of the country crowded into the ranks. The patriotic impulse possessed rich and poor alike. The sons of wealthy men shouldered a musket side by side with the penniless children of toil. Once, by some accident, the money which should have paid a New England regiment failed to arrive in time. A private in the regiment gave his cheque for a hundred thousand dollars, and the men were paid. The Christian churches yielded an earnest support to the war. In some western churches the men enlisted almost without exception. Occasionally their ministers accompanied them. Sabbath-school teachers and members of young men's Christian associations were remarkable for the eagerness with which they obeyed the call of their country. It was no longer a short war and an easy victory which the North anticipated. The gigantic character of the struggle was at length recognized; and the North, chastened, but undismayed, made preparations for a contest on the issue of which her existence depended.

III.

THE YOUNG NAPOLEON.

General M‘Dowell had led the Northern army to a defeat which naturally shook public confidence in his ability to command. A new general was indispensable. When the war broke out, a young man—George B. M‘Clellan by name—was resident in Cincinnati, peacefully occupied with the management of a railroad. He was trained at West Point, and had some reputation for soldiership. Several years before, Mr. Cobden was told by Jefferson Davis that M‘Clellan was one of the best generals the country possessed. He was skilful to construct and organize. His friends knew that he would mould into an army the enthusiastic levies which flowed in; and also that, in obedience to the strongest impulses of his nature, he would shrink from subjecting his army to the supreme test of battle. As a railway man, it was jocularly remarked to Mr. Lincoln, by one who knew him, he was taught to avoid collisions. It was said he built bridges noticeable for their excellence, but could never without discomposure witness trains pass over them. This infirmity of character, hitherto harmless, he was now to carry into a position where it should inflict bitter disappointment upon a great people, and prolong the duration of a bloody and expensive war.

General M‘Clellan was appointed to the command of the army a few days after the defeat at Bull Run. Sanguine hopes were entertained that " the young Napoleon," as he was styled, would give the people victory over their enemies. He addressed himself at once to his task. From every State in the North men hastened to his standard. He disciplined them and perfected their equipment for the field. In October he was at the head of 200,000 men—the largest army ever yet seen on the American continent.

The rebel Government, which at first chose for its home the city of Montgomery in Alabama, moved to Richmond so soon as Virginia gave in her reluctant adherence to the secession cause. Richmond, the gay capital of the Old Dominion, sits queen-like upon a lofty plateau, with deep valleys flanking her on east and west, and the James river rushing past far below upon the south—not many miles from the point where the "dissolute" fathers of the colony had established themselves two centuries and a half ago. To Washington the distance is only one hundred and thirty miles. The warring Governments were within a few hours' journey of each other.

The supreme command of the rebel forces was committed to General Robert E. Lee—one of the greatest of modern soldiers. He was a calm, thoughtful, unpretending man, whose goodness gained for him universal love. He was opposed to secession, but believing, like the rest, that he owed allegiance wholly to his own State, he seceded with Virginia. It was his difficult task to contend nearly always with forces stronger than his own, and to eke out by his own skill and genius the scanty resources of the Confederacy. His consummate ability maintained the war long after all hope of success was gone; and when at length he laid down his arms, even the country against which he had fought was proud of her erring but noble son.

Thomas Jackson—better known as "Stonewall Jackson"—was the most famous of Lee's generals. In him we have a strange evidence of the influence which slavery exerts upon the best of men. He was of truly heroic mould—brave, generous, devout. His military perception was unerring; his decision swift as lightning. He rose early in the morning to read the Scriptures and pray. He gave a tenth part of his income for religious uses. He taught a Sunday class of negro children. He delivered lectures on the authenticity of Scripture. When he dropped a letter into the post-office, he prayed for a blessing on the person to whom it was addressed. As his soldiers marched past his erect, unmoving figure, to meet the enemy, they saw his lips move, and knew that their leader was praying for them to Him who "covereth the head in the day of battle." And yet this good man caused his negroes—male and female—to be flogged when he judged that severity needful. And yet he recommended that the South should "take no prisoners"—in other words, that enemies who had ceased to resist should be massacred. To the end of his life he remained of opinion that the rejection of this policy was a mistake. So fatally do the noblest minds become tainted by the associations of slave society.

During the autumn and early winter of 1861 the weather was unusually fine, and the roads were consequently in excellent condition for the march of an army. The rebel forces were scattered about Virginia— some of them within sight of Washington. Around Richmond it was understood there were few troops. It seemed easy for M'Clellan, with his magnificent army, to trample down any slight resistance which could be offered, and march into the rebel capital. For many weeks the people and the Government waited patiently. They had been too hasty before. They would not again urge their general prematurely into battle. But the months of autumn passed, and no blow was struck. Winter was upon them, and still "all was quiet on the Potomac." M'Clellan, in a series of brilliant reviews, presented his splendid army to the admiration of his countrymen; but he was not yet ready to fight. The country bore the delay for six months. Then it could be endured no longer, and in

January Mr. Lincoln issued a peremptory order that a movement against the enemy should be made. M'Clellan had now laid upon him the necessity to do something. He formed a plan of operations, and by the end of March was ready to begin his work.

South-eastward from Richmond the James and the York rivers fall into the Potomac at a distance from each other of some twenty miles. The course of the rivers is nearly parallel, and the region between them is known as the Peninsula. M'Clellan conveyed his army down the Potomac, landed at Fortress Monroe, and prepared to march upon Richmond by way of the Peninsula.

Before him lay the little town of Yorktown—where, eighty years before, the War of Independence was closed by the surrender of the English army. Yorktown was held by 11,000 rebels. M'Clellan had over 100,000 well-disciplined men eager for battle. But he dared not assault the place, and he wasted a precious month and many precious lives in digging trenches and erecting batteries that he might formally besiege Yorktown. The rebels waited till he was ready to open his batteries, and then quietly marched away. M'Clellan telegraphed to the President that he had gained a brilliant success.

And then M'Clellan crept slowly up the Peninsula. In six weeks he was within a few miles of Richmond, and in front of the forces which the rebels had been actively collecting for the defence of their capital. His army was eager to fight. Lincoln never ceased to urge him to active measures. M'Clellan was immovable. He complained of the weather. He was the victim of "an abnormal season." He telegraphed for more troops. He wrote interminable letters upon the condition of the country. But he would not fight. The emboldened rebels attacked him. The disheartened general thought himself outnumbered, and prepared to retreat. He would retire to the James river and be safe under the protection of the gunboats.

He doubted whether he might not be overwhelmed as he withdrew. If he could not save his army, he would "at least die with it, and share its fate."

Under the influence of such feelings M'Clellan moved away from the presence of a greatly inferior enemy the splendid army of the North, burning with shame and indignation. The rebels dashed at his retreating ranks. His march to the James river occupied seven days. On every day there was a battle. Nearly always the Federals had the advantage in the fight. Always after the fight they resumed their retreat. Once they drove back the enemy—inflicting upon him a crushing defeat. Their hopes rose with success, and they demanded to be led back to Richmond. Nothing is more certain than that at that moment, as indeed during the whole campaign, the rebel capital lay within M'Clellan's grasp. The Hour had come, but not the Man. The army was strong enough for its task, but the general was too weak. M'Clellan shunned the great enterprise which opened before him, and never rested from his inglorious march till he lay in safety, sheltered by the gunboats on the James river. He had lost 15,000 men; but the rebels had suffered even more. It was said that the retreat was skilfully conducted, but the American people were in no humour to appreciate the merits of a chief who was great only in flight. Their disappointment was intense. The Southern leaders devoutly announced "undying gratitude to God" for their great success, and looked forward with increasing confidence to their final triumph over an enemy whose assaults it seemed so easy to repulse.

Nor was this the only success which crowned the rebel arms. The most remarkable battle of the war was fought while the President was vainly endeavouring to rouse M'Clellan to heroic deeds; and it ended in a rebel victory.

At the very beginning of the war the Confederates bethought them of an iron-clad ship of war. They took hold of an old frigate which the Federals had sunk in the James river. They sheathed her in iron plates. They roofed her with iron rails. At her prow, beneath the water-line, they fitted an iron-clad projection, which might be driven into the side of an adversary. They armed her with ten guns of large size.

The mechanical resources of the Confederacy were defective, and this novel structure was eight months in preparation.

1862
A.D.
One morning in March she steamed slowly down the James river, attended by five small vessels of the ordinary sort. A powerful Northern fleet lay guarding the mouth of the river. The *Virginia*—as the iron-clad had been named—came straight towards the hostile ships. She fired no shot. No man showed himself upon her deck. The Federals assailed her with well-aimed discharges. The shot bounded harmless from her sides. She steered for the *Cumberland*, into whose timbers she struck her armed prow. A huge cleft opened in the *Cumberland's* side, and the gallant ship went down with a hundred men of her crew on board. The *Virginia* next attacked the Federal ship *Congress*. At a distance of two hundred yards she opened her guns upon this ill-fated vessel. The *Congress* was aground, and could offer no effective resistance. After sustaining heavy loss, she was forced to surrender. Night approached and the *Virginia* drew off, intending to resume her work on the morrow.

Early next morning—a bright Sunday morning—she steamed out, and made for the *Minnesota*—a Federal ship which had been grounded to get beyond her reach. The *Minnesota* was still aground, and helpless. Beside her, however, as the men on board the *Virginia* observed, lay a mysterious structure, resembling nothing they had ever seen before. Her deck was scarcely visible above the water, and it supported nothing but an iron turret nine feet high. This was the *Monitor*, designed by Captain Ericsson;—the first of the class of iron-clad turret-ships, which are destined, probably, to be the fighting-ships of the future, so long as the world is foolish enough to need ships for fighting purposes. By a singular chance she had arrived thus opportunely. The two iron-clads measured their strength in combat. But their shot produced no impression, and after two hours of heavy but ineffective firing, they separated, and the *Virginia* retired up the James river.

This fight opened a new era in naval warfare. The Washington Government hastened to build turret-ships. All European Governments, perceiving the worthlessness of ships of the old type, proceeded to reconstruct their navies according to the light which the action of the *Virginia* and the *Monitor* afforded them.

The efforts of the North to crush the rebel forces in Virginia had signally failed. But military operations were not confined to Virginia. In this war the battle-field was the continent. Many hundreds of miles from the scene of M'Clellan's feeble efforts, the banner of the Union, held in manlier hands, was advancing into the revolted territory. The North sought to occupy the Border States, and to repossess the line of the Mississippi, thus severing Texas, Louisiana, and Arkansas from the other members of the secession enterprise, and perfecting the blockade which was now effectively maintained on the Atlantic coast. There were troops enough for these vast operations. By the 1st of December 1861, six hundred and forty thousand men had enrolled themselves for the war. The North, thoroughly aroused now, had armed and drilled these enormous hosts. Her foundries worked night and day, moulding cannon and mortars. Her own resources could not produce with sufficient rapidity the gunboats which she needed to assert her supremacy on the Western waters, but she obtained help from the building-yards of Europe. All that wealth and energy could do was done. While the Confederates were supinely trusting to the difficulties of the country and the personal prowess of their soldiers, the North massed forces which nothing on the continent could long resist. In the south and west results were achieved not unworthy of these vast preparations.

During the autumn a strong fleet was sent southward to the Carolina coast. Overcoming with ease the slight resistance which the rebel forts were able to offer, the expedition possessed itself of Port Royal, and thus commanded a large tract of rebel territory. It was a cotton-growing district, worked wholly by slaves. The owners fled, but the slaves remained. The first experiment was made here to prove whether the negro would labour when the lash did not compel. The results were most encouraging. The negroes worked cheerfully and patiently, and many of them became rich from the easy gains of labour on that rich soil.

<small>1861 A.D.</small>

In the west the war was pushed vigorously and with success. To General Grant—a strong, tenacious, silent man, destined ere long to be Commander-in-Chief and President—was assigned the work of driving the rebels out of Kentucky and Tennessee. His gunboats ran up the great rivers of these States and took effective part in the battles which were fought. The rebels were forced southward, till in the spring of 1862 the frontier line of rebel territory no longer enclosed Kentucky. Even Tennessee was held with a loosened and uncertain grasp.

In Arkansas, beyond the Mississippi, was fought the Battle of Pea Ridge, which stretched over three days, and in which the rebels received a sharp defeat. Henceforth the rebels had no footing in Missouri or Arkansas.

<small>March 1862 A.D.</small>

New Orleans fell in April. Admiral Farragut with a powerful fleet forced his way past the forts and gunboats, which composed the insufficient defence of the city. There was no army to resist them. He landed a small party of marines, who pulled down the Secession flag and restored that of the Union. The people looked on silently, while the city passed thus easily away for ever from Confederate rule.

There was gloom in the rebel capital as the tidings of these disasters came in. But the spirit of the people was unbroken, and the Government was encouraged to adopt measures equal to the emergency. A law was enacted which placed at the disposal of the Government every man between eighteen and thirty-five years of age. Enlistment for short terms was discontinued. Henceforth the business of Southern men must be war. Every man must hold himself at his country's call. This law yielded for a time an adequate supply of soldiers, and ushered in those splendid successes which cherished the delusive hope that the slave-power was to establish itself as one of the great powers of the world.

IV.

LIBERTY TO THE CAPTIVE.

The slave question, out of which the rebellion sprang, presented for some time grave difficulties to the Northern Government. As the Northern armies forced their way southwards, escaped slaves flocked to them. These slaves were loyal subjects. Their owners were rebels in arms against the Government. Could the Government recognize the right of the rebel to own the loyal man? Again, the labour of the slaves contributed to the support of the rebellion. Was it not a clear necessity of war that Government should deprive the rebellion of this support by freeing all the slaves whom its authority could reach? But, on the other hand, some of the Slave States remained loyal. Over their slaves Government had no power, and much care was needed that no measure should be adopted of which they could justly complain.

The President had been all his life a steady foe to slavery. But he never forgot that, whatever his own feeling might be, he was strictly bound by law. His duty as President was, not to destroy slavery, but to save the Union. When the time came to overthrow this accursed system, he would do it with gladdened heart. Meanwhile he said, "If I could save the Union without freeing any slave, I would do it; if I could save it by freeing all the slaves, I would do it; and if I could save it by freeing some and leaving others alone, I would do it."

From the very beginning of the war, escaped slaves crowded within the Federal lines. They were willing to perform any labour, or to fight in a cause which they all knew to be their own. But the North was not yet freed from her habitual tenderness for Southern institutions. The negroes could not yet be armed. Nay, it was permitted to the owners of escaped slaves to enter the Northern lines and forcibly to carry back their property. General M'Clellan pledged himself not only to avoid interference with slaves, but to crush with an iron hand any attempt at insurrection on their part. General Fremont, commanding in Missouri, issued an order which gave liberty to the slaves of persons who were fighting against the Union. The President, not yet deeming that measure indispensable, disallowed it. A little later it was proposed to arm the blacks. To that also the President objected. He would do nothing prematurely which might offend the loyal Slave States, and so hinder the restoration of the Union. May 26, **1861** A.D. Aug. 31.

But in War opinion ripens fast. Men quickly learned, under that stern teacher, to reason that, as slavery had caused the rebellion, slavery should be extinguished. Congress met in December, with ideas which pointed decisively towards Abolition. Measures were passed which marked a great era in the history of slavery. The slaves of men who were in arms against the Government were declared to be free. Coloured men might be armed and employed as soldiers. Slavery was abolished within the District of Columbia. Slavery was prohibited for ever within all the Territories. Every slave escaping to the Union armies was to be free. Wherever the authority of Congress could reach, slavery was now at an end.

But something yet remained. Public sentiment in the North grew strong in favour of immediate and unconditional emancipation of all slaves within the revolted States. This view was pressed upon Lincoln. He hesitated long; not from reluctance, but because he wished the public mind to be thoroughly made up before he took this decisive step. At length his course was resolved upon. He drew up a Proclamation, which gave freedom to all the slaves of the rebel States. He called a meeting of his Cabinet, which cordially sanctioned the measure. After New Year's Day of 1863 all persons held to slavery within the seceded territory were declared to be free. "And upon this act"—thus was the Proclamation closed—"sincerely believed to be an act of justice, warranted by the Constitution upon military necessity, I invoke the considerate judgment of mankind, and the gracious favour of Almighty God."

July 1862 A.D.

This—one of the most memorable of all State papers—gave freedom to over three millions of slaves. It did not touch slavery in the loyal States; for there the President had no authority to interfere. But all men knew that it involved the abolition of slavery in the loyal as well as in the rebellious States. Henceforth slavery became impossible on any portion of American territory.

The deep significance of this great measure was most fully recognized by the Northern people. The churches gave thanks to God for this fulfilment of their long-cherished desire. Congress expressed its cordial approval. Innumerable public meetings resolved that the President's action deserved the support of the country. Bells pealed joyfully in the great cities and quiet villages of the East, and in the infant settlements of the distant West. Charles Sumner begged from the President the pen with which the Proclamation had been signed. The original draft of the document was afterwards sold for a large sum, at a fair held in Chicago for the benefit of the soldiers.

The South, too, understood this transaction perfectly. It was the triumphant and final expression of that Northern abhorrence to slavery which had provoked the slave-owners to rebel. It made reconciliation impossible. President Davis said to his

Congress that it would calm the fears of those who apprehended a restoration of the old Union.

It is a painful reflection that the English Government utterly misunderstood this measure. Its official utterance on the subject was a sneer. Earl Russell, the Foreign Secretary of that day, wrote to our Ambassador at Washington that the Proclamation was "a measure of a very questionable kind." "It professes," he continued, "to emancipate slaves where the United States cannot make emancipation a reality, but emancipates no one where the decree can be carried into effect." Thus imperfectly had Earl Russell yet been able to comprehend this memorable page of modern history.

V.

CONFEDERATE SUCCESSES.

M‘Clellan's ignominious failure disappointed but did not dishearten the Northern people. While M‘Clellan was hasting away from Richmond the Governors of seventeen States assured the President of the readiness of their people to furnish troops. The President issued a call for an additional 300,000 men; and his call was promptly obeyed.

M‘Clellan lay for two months, secure but inglorious, beside his gun-boats on the James river. General Lee, rightly deeming that there was little to fear from an army so feebly led, ranged northwards with a strong force and threatened Washington. The Federal troops around the capital were greatly inferior in number. President Lincoln summoned M‘Clellan northwards. M‘Clellan was, as usual, unready; and a small Federal army under General Pope was left to cope unaided with the enemy. Pope received a severe defeat at Manassas, and retired to the fortifications of Washington.

General Lee was strong enough now to carry the war into Northern territory. He captured Harper's Ferry, and passed into Maryland. M‘Clellan was at length stimulated to action, and having carried his troops northwards, he attacked Lee at Antietam. The Northern army far outnumbered the enemy. The battle was long and bloody. When darkness sank down upon the wearied combatants no decisive advantage had been gained. M‘Clellan's

Sept. 17,
1862
A.D.

generals urged a renewal of the attack next morning. But this was not done, and General Lee crossed the Potomac and retired unmolested into Virginia. M'Clellan resumed his customary inactivity. The President ordered him to pursue the enemy and give battle. He even wished him to move on Richmond, which he was able to reach before Lee could possibly be there. In vain. M'Clellan could not move. His horses had sore tongues and sore backs; they were lame; they were broken down by fatigue. Lincoln had already been unduly patient. But the country would endure no more. General M'Clellan was removed from command of that army whose power he had so long been able to neutralize; and his place was taken by General Burnside.

Nov. 5, 1862 A.D.

Burnside at once moved his army southwards. It was not yet too late for a Virginian campaign. He reached the banks of the Rappahannock, beside the little town of Fredericksburg. He had to wait there for many weary days till he obtained means to cross the river. While he lay, impatient, General Lee concentrated all the forces under his command upon the heights which rose steeply from the opposite bank of the stream. He threw up earth-works and strongly intrenched his position. There he waited in calmness for the assault which he knew he could repel.

When Burnside was able to cross the Rappahannock he lost no time in making his attack. One portion of his force would strike the enemy on his right flank; the rest would push straight up the heights and assault him in front. A slight success in his flanking movement cheered General Burnside. But in the centre his troops advanced to the attack under a heavy fire of artillery which laid many brave men low. The Northern soldiers fought their way with steady courage up the height. They were superior in numbers, but the rebels fought in safety within a position which was impregnable. The battle was no fair trial of skill and courage, but a useless waste of brave lives. Burnside drew off his troops and re-crossed the Rappahannock, with a loss of 12,000 men—vainly sacrificed in the attempt to perform an impossibility.

In the West there had been no great success to counterbalance the long train of Confederate victories in the East. The year closed darkly upon the hopes of those who strove to preserve the Union. The South counted with certainty that her independence was secure. The prevailing opinion of Europe regarded the enterprise which the North pursued so resolutely, as a wild impossibility. But the Northern people and Government never despaired of the Commonwealth. At the gloomiest period of the contest a Bill was passed for the construction of a railroad to the Pacific. The Homestead Act offered a welcome to immigrants in the form of a free grant of 160 acres of land to each. And the Government, as with a quiet and unburdened mind, began to enlarge and adorn its Capitol on a scale worthy of the expected greatness of the reunited country.

VI.

THE WAR CONTINUES.

HITHERTO the men who had fought for the North had been volunteers. They had come when the President called, willing to lay down their lives for their country. Already volunteers had been enrolled to the number of one million and a quarter. But that number had been sadly reduced by wounds, sickness, and captivity, and the Northern armies had not proved themselves strong enough to crush the rebellion. A Bill was now passed which subjected the entire male population, between eighteen and forty-five, to military duty when their service was required. Any man of suitable age could now be forced into the ranks.

1863
A.D.

The blockade of the Southern ports had effected for many months an almost complete isolation of the Confederates from the world outside. Now and then a ship, laden with arms and clothing and medicine, ran past the blockading squadron, and discharged her precious wares in a Southern port. Now and then a ship laden with cotton stole out and got safely to sea. But this perilous and scanty commerce afforded no appreciable relief to the want which had already begun to brood over this doomed people. The Government could find soldiers enough; but it could not find for them arms and clothing. The railroads could not be kept in working condition in the absence of foreign iron. Worst of all, a scarcity of food began to threaten. Jefferson Davis begged his people to lay aside all thought of gain, and devote themselves to the raising of supplies for the army. Even now the army was frequently on half supply of bread. The South could look back with just pride upon a long train of brilliant victories, gained with scanty means, by her own valour and genius. But, even in this hour of triumph, it was evident that her position was desperate.

April 10, 1863 A.D.

The North had not yet completely established her supremacy upon the Mississippi. Two rebel strongholds—Vicksburg and Port Hudson—had successfully resisted Federal attack, and maintained communication between the revolted provinces on either side the great river. The reduction of these was indispensable. General Grant was charged with the important enterprise, and proceeded in February to begin his work.

Grant found himself with his army on the wrong side of the city. He was up stream from Vicksburg, and he could not hope to win the place by attacks on that side. Nor could he easily convey his army and siege appliances through the swamps and lakes which stretched away behind the city. It seemed too hazardous to run his transports past the guns of Vicksburg. He attempted to cut a new channel for the river, along which he might convey his army safely. Weeks were spent in the vain attempt, and the country, which had not yet learned to trust in Grant, became impatient of the unproductive toil. Grant, undismayed by the failure of his project, adopted a new and more hopeful scheme. He conveyed his soldiers across to the western bank of the Mississippi, and marched them southward till they were below Vicksburg. There they were ferried across the river; and then they stood within reach of the weakest side of the city. The transports were ordered to run the batteries of Vicksburg and take the chances of that enterprise.

When Grant reached the position he sought he had a difficult task before him. One large army held Vicksburg. Another large army was gathering for the relief of the endangered fortress. Soon Grant lay between two armies which, united, greatly outnumbered his. But he had no intention that they should unite. He attacked them in detail. In every action he was successful. The Confederates were driven back upon the city, which was then closely invested.

For six weeks Grant pressed the siege with a fiery energy which allowed no rest to the besieged. General Johnston was not far off, mustering an army for the relief of Vicksburg, and there was not an hour to lose. Grant kept a strict blockade upon the scantily-provisioned city. From his gun-boats and from his own lines he maintained an almost ceaseless bombardment. The inhabitants crept into caves in the hill to find shelter from the intolerable fire. They slaughtered their mules for food. They patiently endured the inevitable hardships of their position; and their daily newspaper, printed on scraps of such paper as men cover their walls with, continued to the end to make light of their sufferings, and to breathe defiance against General Grant. But all was vain. On the 4th of July—the anniversary of Independence—Vicksburg was surrendered with her garrison of 23,000, men much enfeebled by hunger and fatigue.

The fall of Vicksburg was the heaviest blow which the Confederacy had yet sustained. Nearly one-half of the rebel territory lay beyond the Mississippi. That river was now firmly held by the Federals. The rebel States were cut in two, and no help could pass from one section to the other. There was deep joy in the Northern heart. The President thanked General Grant for "the almost inestimable service" which he had done the country.

But long before Grant's triumph at Vicksburg another humiliation had fallen upon the Federal arms in Virginia.

Soon after the disaster at Fredericksburg, the modest Burnside had asked to be relieved of his command. General Hooker took his place. The new chief was familiarly known to his countrymen as "fighting Joe Hooker,"—a title which sufficiently indicated his dashing, reckless character. Hooker entered on his command with high hopes. "By the blessing of God," he said to the army, "we will contribute something to the renown of our arms and the success of our cause."

After three months of preparation, General Hooker announced that his army was irresistible. The Northern cry was still, "On to Richmond." The dearest wish of the Northern people was to possess the rebel capital. Hooker marched southward, nothing doubting that he was to fulfil the long frustrated desire of his countrymen. His confidence seemed not to be unwarranted; for he had under his command a magnificent army, which greatly outnumbered that opposed to him. But, unhappily for Hooker, the hostile forces were led by General Lee and Stonewall Jackson.

On the 1st of May, Hooker was in presence of the enemy on the line of the Rappahannock. Lee was too weak to give or accept battle; but he was able to occupy Hooker with a series of sham attacks. All the while Jackson was hasting to assail his flank. His march was through the Wilderness—a wild country thick with ill-grown oaks and a dense undergrowth—where surprise was easy. Towards evening, on the 2nd, Jackson's soldiers burst upon the unexpectant Federals. The fury of the attack bore all before it. The Federal line fell back in confusion and with heavy loss.

In the twilight Jackson rode forward with his staff to examine the enemy's position. As he returned, a North Carolina regiment, seeing a party of horsemen approach, presumed it was a charge of Federal cavalry. They fired, and Jackson fell from his horse, with two bullets in his left arm and one through his right hand. They placed him on a litter to carry him from the field. One of the bearers was shot down by the enemy, and the wounded general fell heavily to the ground. The sound of musketry wakened the Federal artillery, and for some time Jackson lay helpless on ground swept by the cannon of the enemy. When his men learned the situation of their beloved commander, they rushed in and carried him from the danger.

Jackson sunk under his wounds. He bore patiently his great suffering. "If I live, it will be for the best," he said; "and if I die, it will be for the best. God knows and directs all things for the best." He died eight days after the battle, to the deep sorrow of his countrymen. He was a great soldier; and although he died fighting for an evil cause, he was a true-hearted Christian man.

During two days after Jackson fell the battle continued at Chancellorsville. Lee's superior skill in command more than compensated for his inferior numbers. He attacked Hooker, and always at the point of conflict he was found to be stronger. Hooker discovered that he must retreat, lest a worse thing should befall him. After three days' fighting he crossed the river in a tempest of wind and rain, and along the muddy Virginian roads carried his disheartened troops back to their old positions. He had been baffled by a force certainly not more than one-half his own. The splendid military genius of Lee was perhaps never more conspicuous than in the defeat of that great army which General Hooker himself regarded as invincible.

VII.

GETTYSBURG.

The Confederate Government had always been eager to carry the contest into Northern territory. It was satisfying to the natural pride of the South, and it was thought that some experience of the evils of war might incline the Northern mind to peace. Lee was ordered to march into Pennsylvania. He gathered all the troops at his disposal, and with 75,000 men he crossed the Potomac, and was once more prepared to face the enemy on his own soil. The rich cities of the North trembled. It was not unlikely that he should possess himself of Baltimore and Philadelphia. Could he once again defeat Hooker's army, as he had often done before, no further resistance was possible. Pennsylvania and New York were at his mercy.

Lee advanced to the little Pennsylvanian town of Gettysburg. Hooker, after marching his army northwards, had been relieved of the command. A battle was near; and in face of the enemy a new commander had to be chosen. Two days before the hostile armies met, General Meade was appointed. Meade was an experienced soldier, who had filled with honour the various positions assigned to him. It was seemingly a hopeless task which he was now asked to perform. With an oft-defeated army of 60,000 to 70,000 men, to whom he was a stranger, he had to meet Lee with his victorious 75,000. Meade quietly undertook the work appointed to him, and did it, too, like a brave, prudent unpretending man.

The battle lasted for three days. On the first day the Confederates had some advantage. Their attack broke and scattered a Federal division with considerable loss. But that night the careful Meade took up a strong position on a crescent-shaped line of heights near the little town. Here he would lie, and the Confederates might drive him from it if they could.

July 1, **1863** A.D.

Next day Lee attempted to dislodge the enemy. The key of the Federal position was Cemetery Hill, and there the utmost strength of the Confederate attack was put forth. Nor was it in vain. Part of the Federal line was broken. At one point an important position had been taken by the Confederates. Lee might fairly hope that another day's fighting would complete his success and give him undisputed possession of the wealthiest Northern States. His loss had been small, while the Federals had been seriously weakened.

July 2.

Perhaps no hours of deeper gloom were ever passed in the North than the hours of that summer evening when the telegraph flashed over the country the news of Lee's success. The lavish sacrifice of blood and treasure seemed in vain. A million of men were in arms to defend the Union, and yet the northward progress of the rebels could not be withstood. Should Lee be victorious on the morrow, the most hopeful must despond.

The day on which so much of the destiny of America hung opened bright and warm and still. The morning was occupied by Lee in preparations for a crushing attack upon the centre of the Federal position; by Meade, in carefully strengthening his power of resistance at the point where he was to win or to lose this decisive battle. About noon all was completed. Over both armies there fell a marvellous stillness—the silence of anxious and awful expectation. It was broken by a solitary cannon-shot, and the shriek of a Whitworth shell as it rushed through the air. That was the signal

July 3.

at which one hundred and fifty Confederate guns opened their fire. The Federal artillery replied. For three hours a prodigious hail of shells fell upon either army. No decisive supremacy was, however, established by the guns on either side, although heavy loss was sustained by both. While the cannonade still continued, Lee sent forth the columns whose errand it was to break the Federal centre. They marched down the low range of heights on which they had stood, and across the little intervening valley. As they moved up the opposite height the friendly shelter of Confederate fire ceased. Terrific discharges of grape and shell smote but did not shake their steady ranks. As the men fell their comrades stepped into their places, and the undismayed lines moved swiftly on. Up to the low stone wall which sheltered the Federals, up to the very muzzles of guns whose rapid fire cut every instant deep lines in their ranks, the heroic advance was continued.

General Lee from the opposite height watched, as Napoleon did at Waterloo, the progress of his attack. Once the smoke of battle was for a moment blown aside, and the Confederate flag was seen to wave within the enemy's position. Lee's generals congratulate him that the victory is gained. Again the cloud gathers around the combatants. When it lifts next, the Confederates are seen broken and fleeing down that fatal slope, where a man can walk now without once putting his foot upon the grass, so thick lie the bodies of the slain. The attack had failed. The battle was lost. The Union was saved.

General Lee's business was now to save his army. "This has been a sad day for us," he said to a friend, "a sad day; but we can't expect always to gain victories." He rallied his broken troops, expecting to be attacked by the victorious Federals. But Meade did not follow up his success. Next day Lee began his retreat. In perfect order he moved towards the Potomac, and safely crossed the swollen river back into Virginia.

The losses sustained in this battle were terrible. Forty-eight thousand men lay dead or wounded on the field. Lee's army was weakened by over 40,000 men killed, wounded, and prisoners. Meade lost 23,000. For miles around, every barn, every cottage contained wounded men. The streets of the little town were all dabbled with blood. Men were for many days engaged in burying the dead, of whom there were nearly 8000. The wounded of both armies, who were able to be removed, were at once carried into hospitals and tenderly cared for. There were many so mangled that their removal was impossible. These were ministered to on the field till death relieved them from their pain.

The tidings of the victory at Gettysburg came to the Northern people on the 4th of July, side by side with the tidings of the fall of Vicksburg. The proud old anniversary had perhaps never before been celebrated by the American people with hearts so thankful and so glad. Mr. Lincoln, who had become grave and humble and reverential under the influence of those awful circumstances amid which he lived, proclaimed a solemn day of thanksgiving for the deliverance granted to the nation, and of prayer that God would lead them all, " through the paths of repentance and submission to the divine will, to unity and fraternal peace."

The deep enthusiasm which, in those anxious days, thrilled the American heart, sought in song that fulness of expression which speech could not afford. Foremost among the favourite poetic utterances of the people was this :—

BATTLE-HYMN OF THE REPUBLIC.

Mine eyes have seen the glory of the coming of the Lord;
He is trampling out the vintage where the grapes of wrath are stored;
He hath loosed the fateful lightning of His terrible swift sword;
   His Truth is marching on.

> I have seen Him in the watch-fires of a hundred circling camps;
> They have builded Him an altar in the evening dews and damps;
> I have read His righteous sentence by the dim and flaring lamps;
>   His Day is marching on.
>
> I have read a fiery gospel writ in burnished rows of steel—
> "As ye deal with My contemners, so with you My grace shall deal;"
> Let the Hero born of woman crush the serpent with His heel,
>   Since God is marching on.
>
> He has sounded forth the trumpet that shall never call retreat;
> He is sifting out the hearts of men before His judgment-seat;
> Oh! be swift, my soul, to answer Him; be jubilant, my feet,—
>   Our God is marching on.
>
> In the beauty of the lilies Christ was born across the sea,
> With a glory in His bosom that transfigures you and me;
> As He died to make men holy, let us die to make men free,
>   While God is marching on.

These strangely musical verses were sung at all public meetings in the North, the audience ordinarily starting to their feet and joining in the strain, often interrupted by emotion too deeply stirred to be concealed. President Lincoln has been seen listening to the hymn with tears rolling down his face. When the Battle of Gettysburg was fought there were many hundreds of Northern officers captive in the Libby prison—a huge, shapeless structure, once a tobacco factory, standing by the wayside in a suburb of Richmond. A false report was brought to them that the rebels had gained. There were many sleepless eyes and sorrowing hearts that night among the prisoners. But next morning an old negro brought them the true account of the battle. The sudden joy was too deep for words. By one universal impulse the gladdened captives burst into song. Midst weeping and midst laughter the Battle-Hymn of the Republic was caught up until five hundred voices were joining in the strain. There as elsewhere it was felt with unutterable joy and thankfulness that the country was saved.

The victory at Gettysburg lifted a great load from the hearts of the Northern people. There was yet a work—vast and grim—to be accomplished before a solid peace could be attained. But there was now a sure hope of final success. It was remarked by President Lincoln's friends that his appearance underwent a noticeable change after Gettysburg. His eye grew brighter; his bowed-down form was once more erect. In the winter after the battle part of the battle-ground was consecrated as a cemetery, into which were gathered the remains of the brave men who fell. Lincoln took part in the ceremony, and spoke these memorable words: "It is for us the living to be dedicated here to the unfinished work which they who fought here have thus far so nobly advanced. It is for us to be here dedicated to the great task remaining before us; that from these honoured dead we take increased devotion to that cause for which they gave the last full measure of devotion; that we here highly resolve that these dead shall not have died in vain; that this nation, under God, shall have a new birth of freedom; and that government of the people—by the people and for the people—shall not perish from the earth."

VIII.

THE LAST CAMPAIGN.

Even before the disasters of Gettysburg and Vicksburg, and while General Lee was still pursuing a course of dazzling success, it had become evident to many that the cause of the South was hopeless. A strict blockade shut her out from the markets of Europe. Her supplies of arms were running so low, that even if she could have found men in sufficient numbers to resist the North, she could not have equipped them. Food was becoming scarce. Already the pangs of hunger had been experienced in Lee's army. Elsewhere there was much suffering, even among those who had lately been rich. The soldiers were insufficiently provided with clothing. As winter came on they deserted and went home in crowds so great that punishment was impossible.

The North had a million of men in the field. She had nearly six hundred ships of war, seventy-five of which were iron-clads. She had boundless command of everything which could contribute to the efficiency and comfort of her soldiers. The rolls of the Southern armies showed only four hundred thousand men under arms, and of these it was said that from desertion and other causes seldom more than one-half were in the ranks.

Money was becoming very scarce. The Confederate Government borrowed all the money it could at home. But the supply received was wholly out of proportion to the expenditure. A loan was attempted in England, and there proved to be there a sufficient number of rich but unwise persons to furnish three millions sterling—most of which will remain for ever unpaid to the lenders. No other measure remained but to print, as fast as machinery would do it, Government promises to pay at some future time, and to force these upon people to whom the Government owed money. These promises gradually fell in value. In 1862, when the rebellion was young and hopes were high, one dollar and twenty cents in Government money would purchase a dollar in gold. In January 1863 it required three dollars to do that. After Gettysburg it required twenty dollars. Somewhat later it required sixty paper dollars to obtain the one precious golden coin.

It became every day more apparent that the resources of the South were being exhausted. Even if the genius of her generals should continue to gain victories, the South must perish from want of money and want of food. There was a touching weakness in many of her business arrangements. Government appealed to the people for gifts of jewellery and silver plate, and published in the Richmond newspapers lists of the gold rings and silver spoons and teapots which amiable enthusiasts bestowed upon them! When iron-clad ships of war were needed and iron was scarce, an association of ladies was formed to collect old pots and pans for the purpose! The daring of these people and the skill of their leaders might indeed gain them victories; but it was a wild improbability that they should come successfully out of a war in which the powerful and sagacious North was resolute to win.

The Northern Government, well advised of the failing resources of the South, hoped that one campaign more would close the war. Bitter experience had corrected their early mistakes. They had at length found a general worthy of his high place. Grant was summoned eastward to direct the last march on Richmond. The spirit of the country was resolute as ever. The soldiers had now the skill of

1864 A.D.

veterans. Enormous supplies were provided. Everything that boundless resources, wisely administered, could do, was now done to bring the awful contest to a close.

When the campaign opened, Grant with 120,000 men faced Lee, whose force was certainly less by one-half. The little river Rapidan flowed between. The Wilderness—a desolate region of stunted trees and dense undergrowth—stretched for many miles around. At midnight, on the 3rd of May, Grant began to cross the river, and before next evening his army stood on the southern side. Lee at once attacked him. During the next eight days there was continuous fighting. The men toiled all day at the work of slaughter, lay down to sleep at night, and rose to resume their bloody labour in the morning, as men do in the ordinary peaceful business of life. Lee directed his scanty force with wondrous skill. It was his habit to throw up intrenchments, within which he maintained himself against the Federal assault. Grant did not allow himself to be hindered in his progress to Richmond. When he failed to force the Confederate position he marched southward round its flank, continually obliging Lee to move forward and take up a new position. His losses were terrible. From the 5th to the 12th of May he had lost 30,000 men in killed, wounded, and missing. The wounded were sent to Washington. Trains of ambulances miles in length, laden with suffering men, passed continually through the capital, filling all hearts with sadness and gloomy apprehension. The cost was awful, but General Grant knew that the end was being gained. He knew that Lee was weakened irrecoverably by the slaughter of these battles, and he wrote that he would "fight it out on this line, if it should take all summer."

Grant found that a direct attack on Richmond was as yet hopeless. He marched southwards past the rebel capital to the little town of Petersburg, twenty-two miles off. His plan was to wear down the rebel army by the continual attack of superior forces, and also to cut the railways by which provisions were brought into Richmond. By the middle of June he was before Petersburg, which he hoped to possess before Lee had time to fortify the place against him. It might have been taken by a vigorous assault, but the attacking force was feebly led, and the opportunity was missed.

And now there began the tedious bloody siege of Petersburg. The armies had chosen their positions for the final conflict. The result was not doubtful. General Lee was of opinion, some time ago, that the fortunes of the Confederacy were desperate. The Northern Government and military leaders knew that success was certain. Indeed General Grant stated afterwards that he had been at the front from the very beginning of the war, and that he had never entertained any doubt whatever as to the final success of the North.

All around Petersburg, at such distance that the firing did not very seriously affect the little city, stretched the earthworks of the combatants. Before the end there were forty miles of earthworks. The Confederates established a line of defence. The Federals established a line of attack, and gradually, by superior strength, drove their antagonists back. Lee retired to a new series of defences, where the fight was continued. The Federals had a railway running to City Point, eleven miles away, where their ships brought for them the amplest supplies. Lee depended upon the railways which communicated with distant portions of Confederate territory. These it was the aim of Grant to cut, so that his adversary might be driven by want of food from his position. The outposts of the armies were within talking distance of each other. The men lay in rifle-pits or shallow ditches, watching opportunity to kill. Any foe who incautiously came within range died by their unerring fire. For ten long months the daily occupation of the combatants had been to attack each the positions of the other. The Confederates, by constant sallies, attempted to hinder the advance of their powerful assailant. Grant never relaxed his hold. He "had the rebellion by the throat," and he steadily tightened his grasp. By City Point he was in easy communication with the boundless resources of the North. Men and stores were supplied as he needed them by an enthusiastic country. On the rebel side the last available man was now in the field. Half the time the army wanted food. Desertions abounded. It was not that the men shunned danger or hardship, but they knew the cause was hopeless. Many of them knew also that their families were starving. They went home to help those who were dearer to them than that desperate enterprise whose ruin was now so manifest. The genius of Lee was the sole remaining buttress of the Confederate cause.

Once the Federals ran an enormous mine under a portion of the enemy's works. In this mine they piled up twelve thousand pounds of gunpowder. They had a strong column ready to march into the opening which the explosion would cleave. Early one summer morning the mine was fired. A vast mass of earth, mingled with bodies of men, was thrown high into air. The Confederate defence at that point was effaced. The attacking force moved forward. But from some unexplained reason they paused and sheltered themselves in the huge pit formed by the explosion. The Confederates promptly brought up artillery and rained shells into the pit, where soon fifteen hundred men lay dead. The discomfited Federals retired to their lines.

When Grant began his march to Richmond, he took care that the enemy should be pressed in other quarters of his territory. General Sherman marched from Tennessee down into Georgia. Before him was a strong Confederate army and a country peculiarly favourable for an army contented to remain on the defensive. Sherman overcame every obstacle. He defeated his enemy in many battles and bloody skirmishes. His object was to reach Atlanta, the capital of Georgia. Atlanta was of extreme value to the rebels. It commanded railroads which conveyed supplies to their armies. It had great factories where they manufactured cannon and locomotives; great foundries where they laboured incessantly to produce shot and shell. Sherman, by brilliant generalship and hard fighting, overcame all resistance, and entered Atlanta, September 2. It was a great prize, but it was not had cheaply. During these four months he had lost 30,000 men.

When Sherman had held Atlanta for a few weeks he resolved to march eastward through Georgia to the sea. He had a magnificent army of 60,000 men, for whom there was no sufficient occupation where they lay. On the sea-coast there were cities to be taken. And then his army could march northwards to join Grant before Petersburg.

When all was ready Sherman put the torch to the public buildings of Atlanta, telegraphed northwards that all was well, and cut the telegraph wires. Then he started on his march of three hundred miles across a hostile country. For a month nothing was heard of him. When he re-appeared it was before Savannah, of which he quickly possessed himself. His march through Georgia had been unopposed. He severely wasted the country for thirty miles on either side of the line from Atlanta to Savannah. He carried off the supplies he needed. He destroyed what he could not use. He tore up the railroads. He proclaimed liberty to the slaves, many of whom accompanied him eastward. He proved to all the world how hollow a thing was now the Confederacy, and how rapidly its doom was approaching.

Nov. 15, 1864 A.D.

At the north, in the valley of the Shenandoah, a strong Confederate army, under the habitually unsuccessful General Early, confronted the Federals under Sheridan. Could Sheridan have been driven away, the war might again have been carried into Pennsylvania or Maryland, and the North humbled in her career of victory. But Sheridan was still triumphant. At length General Early effected a surprise. He burst upon the Federals while they looked not for him. His sudden attack disordered the enemy, who began to retire. Sheridan was not with his army. He had gone to Winchester, twenty miles away. The morning breeze from the south bore to his startled ear the sounds of battle. Sheridan mounted his horse, and rode with the speed of a man who felt that upon his presence hung the destiny of the fight. His army was on the verge of defeat, and already stragglers were hurrying from the field. But when Sheridan galloped among them, the battle was restored. Under Sheridan the army was invincible. The rebels were defeated with heavy loss, and were never again able to renew the war in the valley of the Shenandoah.

Oct. 19, 1864 A.D.

The Slave question was not yet completely settled. The Proclamation had made free the slaves of all who were rebels, and nothing remained between them and liberty but those thin lines of gray-coated hungry soldiers, upon whose arms the genius of Lee bestowed an efficacy not naturally their own. But the Proclamation had no power to free the slaves of loyal citizens. In the States which had not revolted slavery was the same as it had ever been. The feeling deepened rapidly throughout the North that this could not continue. Slavery had borne fruit in the hugest rebellion known to history. It had proclaimed irreconcilable hostility to the Government. It had brought mourning and woe into every house. The Union could not continue half-slave and half-free. The North wisely and nobly resolved that slavery should cease.

Most of the loyal Slave States freed themselves by their own choice of this evil institution. Louisiana, brought back to her allegiance not without some measure of force, led the way. Maryland followed, and Tennessee, and Missouri, and Arkansas. In Missouri, whence the influence issued which murdered Lovejoy because he was an abolitionist—which supplied the Border ruffians in the early days of Kansas—the abolition of slavery was welcomed with devout prayer and thanksgiving, with joyful illuminations and speeches and patriotic songs.

One thing was yet wanting to the complete and final extinction of slavery. The Constitution permitted the existence of the accursed thing. If the Constitution were so amended as to forbid slavery upon American soil, the cause of this huge discord which now convulsed the land would be removed. A Constitutional Amendment to this effect was submitted to the people. In the early months of 1865, while General Lee—worthy to fight in a better cause—was still bravely toiling to avert the coming doom of the Slave Empire, the Northern States joyfully adopted the Amendment. Slavery was now at length extinct. This was what Providence had mercifully brought out of a rebellion whose avowed object it was to establish slavery more firmly and extend it more widely.

But freedom was not enough. Many of the black men had faithfully served the Union. Nearly two hundred thousand of them were in the ranks—fighting manfully in a cause which was specially their own. There were many black men, as Lincoln said, who "could remember that with silent tongue, and clenched teeth, and steady eye, and well-poised bayonet, they had helped mankind to save liberty in America." But the coloured race was child-like and helpless. They had to be looked upon as "the wards of the nation." A Freedmen's Bureau was established, to be the defence of the defenceless blacks. General Howard—a man peculiarly fitted to give wise effect to the kind purposes of the nation—became the head of this department. It was his duty to provide food and

1864 A.D.

shelter for the slaves who were set free by military operations in the revolted States. He settled them, as he could, on confiscated lands. After a time he had to see to the education of their children. In all needful ways he was to keep the negroes from wrong till they were able to keep themselves.

Four years had now passed since Lincoln's election furnished the slave-owners with a pretext to rebel. Another election had to be made. Lincoln was again proposed as the Republican candidate. The Democratic party nominated M'Clellan—the general who so scrupulously avoided collisions when he commanded a Federal army. The war, said the Democrats, is a failure; let us have a cessation of hostilities, and endeavour to save the Union by peaceful negotiation. Let us put down slavery and rebellion by force, said the Republicans; there is no other way. These were the simple issues on which the election turned. Mr. Lincoln was re-elected by the largest majority ever known. "It is not in my nature," he said, "to triumph over any one; but I give thanks to Almighty God for this evidence of the people's resolution to stand by free government and the rights of humanity."

He was inaugurated according to the usual form. His Address was brief, but high-toned and solemn, as beseemed the circumstances. Perhaps no State paper ever produced so deep an impression upon the American people. It closed thus:—"Fondly do we hope, fervently do we pray, that this mighty scourge of war may speedily pass away. Yet if God wills that it continue until all the wealth piled by the bondsman's two hundred and fifty years of unrequited toil shall be sunk, and until every drop of blood drawn with the lash shall be paid by another drawn with the sword—as was said three thousand years ago, so still it must be said, 'The judgments of the Lord are true and righteous altogether.'

March 4, 1865 A.D.

With malice towards none, with charity for all, with firmness in the right as God gives us to see the right, let us finish the work we are in, to bind up the nation's wounds, to care for him who shall have borne the battle, and for his widow and his orphans—to do all which may achieve and cherish a just and a lasting peace among ourselves and with all nations."

During the winter months it became very plain that the Confederacy was tottering to its fall. These were the bitterest months through which Virginia had ever passed. The army was habitually now on short supply. Occasionally, for a day, there was almost a total absence of food. One day in December Lee telegraphed to Richmond that his army was without meat, and dependent on a little bread. And yet the soldiers were greatly better off than the citizens. Provisions were seized for the army wherever they could be found, and the owners were mercilessly left to starve. The suffering endured among the once cheerful homes of Virginia was terrible.

Every grown man was the property of the Government. It was said the rich men escaped easily. But a poor man could not pass along a street in Richmond without imminent risk of being seized and sent down to the lines at Petersburg. At railroad stations might be constantly seen groups of squalid men on their way to camp—caught up from their homes and hurried off to fight for a cause which they all knew to be desperate—in the service of a Government which they no longer trusted. It was, of course, the earliest care of these men to desert. They went home. They surrendered to the enemy. The spirit which made the Confederacy formidable no longer survived.

General Lee had long before expressed his belief that without the help of the slaves the war must end disastrously. But all men knew that a slave who had been a soldier could be a slave no longer. The owners were not prepared to free their slaves, and they refused therefore to arm them. In November—with utter ruin impending—a Bill was introduced into the Confederate Congress for arming two hundred thousand negroes. It was debated till the following March. Then a feeble compromise was passed, merely giving the President power to accept such slaves as were offered to him. So inflexibly resolute were the leaders of the South in their hostility to emancipation. It was wholly unimportant. At that time Government could have armed only another five thousand men; and could not feed the men it had.

The finances of the Confederacy were an utter wreck. Government itself sold specie at the rate of one gold dollar for sixty dollars in paper money. Mr. Davis, by a measure of partial repudiation, relieved himself for a short space from some of his embarrassments. But no device would gain public confidence for the currency of a falling power. A loaf of bread cost three dollars. It took a month's pay to buy the soldier a pair of stockings. The misery of the country was deep, abject, unutterable. President Davis came to be regarded with abhorrence, as the cause of all this wretchedness. Curses, growing ever deeper and louder, were breathed against the unsuccessful chief.

Feb. 17, 1864 A.D.

General Grant, well aware of the desperate condition of the Confederates, pressed incessantly upon their enfeebled lines. He had 160,000 men under his command. Sheridan joined him with a magnificent force of cavalry. Sherman with his victorious army was near. Grant began to fear that Lee would take to flight, and keep the rebellion alive on other fields. A general movement of all the forces around Richmond was decided upon. Lee struggled bravely, but in vain, against overwhelming numbers. His right was assailed by Sheridan, and driven back with heavy loss—

March 29, 1865 A.D.

5000 hungry and disheartened men laying down their arms. On that same night Grant opened, from all his guns, a terrific and prolonged bombardment. At dawn the assault was made. Its strength was directed against one of the Confederate forts. The fight ceased elsewhere, and the armies looked on. There was a steady advance of the blue-coated lines; a murderous volley from the little garrison; wild cheers from the excited spectators. Under a heavy fire of artillery and musketry the soldiers of the Union rush on; they swarm into the ditch and up the sides of the works. Those who first reach the summit fall back slain by musket-shot or bayonet-thrust. But others press fiercely on. Soon their exulting cheers tell that the fort is won. Lee's army is cut in two. His position is no longer tenable. He telegraphed at once to President Davis that Richmond must be evacuated.

April 1, **1865** A.D.

April 2.

It was Communion Sunday in St. Paul's Episcopal Church, and President Davis was in his pew among the other worshippers. No intelligence from the army had been allowed to reach the public for some days. But the sound of Grant's guns had been heard, and the reserve of the Government was ominous. Many a keen eye sought to gather from the aspect of the President some forecast of the future. In vain. That serene self-possessed face had lost nothing of its habitual reticence. In all that congregation there was no worshipper who seemed less encumbered by the world, more absorbed by the sacred employment of the hour, than President Davis. The service proceeded, and the congregation knelt in prayer. As President Davis rose from his knees the sexton handed him a slip of paper. He calmly read it. Then he calmly lifted his prayer-book, and with unmoved face walked softly from the church. It was Lee's message he had received. Jefferson Davis's sole concern now was to escape the doom of the traitor and the rebel. He fled at once, by special train, towards the south. Then the work of evacuation commenced. The gun-boats on the river were blown up. The bridges were destroyed. The great warehouses in the city were set on fire, and in the flames thus wickedly kindled a third part of the city was consumed. All who had made themselves prominent in the rebellion fled from the anticipated vengeance of the Federals. The soldiers were marched off, plundering as they went. Next morning Richmond was in possession of the Northern troops. Among the first to enter the capital of the rebel slave-owners was a regiment of negro cavalry.

About midnight on Sunday Lee began his retreat from the position which he had kept so well. Grant promptly followed him. On the Tuesday morning Lee reached a point where he had ordered supplies to wait him. By some fatal blunder the cars laden with the food which his men needed so much had been run on to Richmond, and were lost to him. Hungry and weary the men toiled on, hotly pursued by Grant. Soon a hostile force appeared in their front, and it became evident that they were surrounded.

April 4, 1865 A.D.

General Grant wrote to General Lee asking the surrender of his army, to spare the useless effusion of blood. Lee did not at first admit that surrender was necessary, and Grant pressed the pursuit with relentless energy. Lee wrote again to request a meeting, that the terms of surrender might be arranged. The two leaders met in a wayside cottage. They had never seen each other before, although they had both served in the Mexican War, and Lee mentioned pleasantly that he remembered the name of his antagonist from that time. Grant drew up and presented in writing the terms which he offered. The men were to lay down their arms, and give their pledge that they would not serve against the American Government till regularly exchanged. They were then to return to their homes, with a guarantee that

April 7.

April 9.

they would not be disturbed by the Government against which they had rebelled. Grant asked if these terms were satisfactory. "Yes," said Lee, "they are satisfactory. The truth is, I am in such a position that any terms offered to me *must* be satisfactory." And then he told how his men had been for two days without food, and begged General Grant to spare them what he could. Grant, generously eager to relieve his fallen enemies, despatched instantly a large drove of oxen and a train of provision waggons. In half an hour there were heard in the Federal camp the cheers with which the hungry rebels welcomed those precious gifts.

Lee rode quietly back to his army. The surrender was expected. When its details became known, officers and men crowded around their much-loved chief to assure him of their devotion, to obtain a parting grasp of his hand. Lee was too deeply moved to say much. "Men," he said, with his habitual simplicity, "we have fought through the war together, and I have done the best I could for you." A day or two later the men stacked their arms and went to their homes. The history of the once splendid Army of Northern Virginia had closed.

Lee's surrender led the way to the surrender of all the Confederate armies. Within a few days there was no organized force of any importance in arms against the Union. The War of the Great Rebellion was at an end.

IX.

THE MURDER OF THE PRESIDENT.

WHEN the closing operations against Richmond were being arranged, President Lincoln went down to General Grant's head-quarters at City Point. He remained there till Lee's surrender. He visited Richmond on the day it was taken, and walked through the streets with his little boy in his hand. The freed slaves crowded to welcome their deliverer. They expressed in a thousand grotesque ways their gratitude to the good "Father Abraham." There had been dark hints for some time that there were those among the Confederates who would avenge their defeat by the murder of the President. Mr. Lincoln was urged to be on his guard, and his friends were unwilling that he should visit Richmond. He himself cared little, now that the national cause had triumphed.

He returned unharmed to Washington on the evening of Lee's surrender. The next few days were perhaps the brightest in his whole life. He had guided the nation through the heaviest trial which had ever assailed it. On every side were joy and gladness. Flags waved, bells rang, guns were fired, houses were lighted up; the thanks of innumerable grateful hearts went up to God for this great deliverance. No heart in all the country was more joyful and more thankful than Mr. Lincoln's. He occupied himself with plans for healing the wounds of his bleeding country, and bringing back the revolted States to a contented occupation of their appointed places

April 9,
1865
A.D.

in the Union. No thought of severity was in his mind. Now that armed resistance to the Government was crushed, the gentlest measures which would give security in the future were the measures most agreeable to the good President.

On the 14th he held a meeting of his Cabinet, at which General Grant was present. The quiet cheerfulness and hopefulness of the President imparted to the proceedings of the council a tone long remembered by those who were present. After the meeting he drove out with Mrs. Lincoln, to whom he talked of the good days in store. They had had a hard time, he said, since they came to Washington; but now, by God's blessing, they might hope for quieter and happier years.

In the evening he drove, with Mrs. Lincoln and two or three friends, to a theatre where he knew the people expected his coming. As the play went on the audience were startled by a pistol-shot in the President's box. A man brandishing a dagger was seen to leap from the box on to the stage, and with a wild cry—" The South is avenged!"—disappeared behind the scenes. The President sat motionless, his head sunk down upon his breast. He was evidently unconscious. When the surgeon came, it was found that a bullet had pierced the brain, inflicting a deadly wound. He was carried to a house close by. His family and the great officers of State, by whom he was dearly loved, sat around the bed of the dying President. He lingered till morning, breathing heavily, but in entire unconsciousness, and then he passed away.

At the same hour the President was murdered a ruffian broke into the sick-room of Mr. Seward, who was suffering from a recent accident, and stabbed him almost to death as he lay in bed. His bloody work was happily interrupted, and Mr. Seward recovered.

The assassin of Mr. Lincoln was an actor called Booth, a fanatical adherent of the fallen Confederacy. His leg was broken in the leap on to the stage, but he was able to reach a horse which stood ready at the theatre door. He rode through the city, crossed the Potomac by a bridge, in the face of the sentinels posted there, and passed safely beyond present pursuit. A week later he was found hid in a barn, and well armed. He refused to surrender, and was preparing to fire, when a soldier ended his miserable existence by a bullet.

The grief of the American people for their murdered President was beyond example deep and bitter. Perhaps for no man were there ever shed so profusely the tears of sorrow. Not in America alone, but in England too—where President Lincoln was at length understood and honoured—his loss was deeply mourned. It was resolved that he should be buried beside his old home in Illinois. The embalmed remains were to be conveyed to their distant resting-place by a route which would give to the people of the chief Northern cities a last opportunity to look upon the features of the man they loved so well. The sad procession moved on its long journey of nearly two thousand miles, traversing the States of Maryland, Pennsylvania, New Jersey, New York, Ohio, Indiana, and Illinois. Everywhere, as the funeral train passed, the weeping people sought to give expression to their reverential sorrow. At the great cities the body lay in state, and all business was suspended.

At length Springfield was reached. The body was taken to the State House. His neighbours looked once more upon that well-remembered face, wasted, indeed, by years of anxious toil, but wearing still, as of old, its kind and placid expression.

Four years ago Lincoln said to his neighbours, when he was leaving them, "I know not how soon I shall see you again. I go to assume a task more difficult than that which has devolved upon any other man since the days of Washington." He had nobly accomplished his task; and this was the manner of his home-coming.

X.

THE LOSSES AND THE GAINS OF THE WAR.

THE Great Rebellion was at an end. It was not closed by untimely concessions which left a discontented party, with its strength unbroken, ready to renew the contest at a more fitting time. It was fought out to the bitter end. The slave-power might be erring, but it was not weak. The conflict was closed by the utter exhaustion of one of the combatants. Lee did not surrender till his army was surrounded by the enemy and had been two days without food. The great questions which had been appealed to the sword were answered conclusively and for ever.

The cost had been very terrible. On the Northern side, two million seven hundred thousand men bore arms at some period of the war. Of these there died in battle, or in hospital of wounds received in battle, ninety-six thousand men. There died in hospital of disease, one hundred and eighty-four thousand. Many went home wounded, to die among the scenes of their infancy. Many went home stricken with lingering and mortal disease. Of these there is no record but in the sad memories which haunt nearly every Northern home.

The losses on the Southern side have not been accurately ascertained. The white population of the revolted States numbered about a fourth of the loyal Northern population. At the close of the war the North had a full million of men under arms. The Southern armies which surrendered numbered one hundred and seventy-five thousand. When to this is added the number who went home without awaiting the formality of surrender, it appears probable that the Southern armies bore to the Northern the same proportion that the population did. Presumably the loss bore a larger proportion, as the deaths from disease, owing to the greater hardships to be endured, must have been excessive in the rebel army. It must be under the truth to say that one hundred and fifty thousand Southerners perished in the field or in the hospital.

The war cost the North in money seven hundred millions sterling. It is impossible to state what was the cost to the South. The Confederate debt was supposed to amount at the close to thirty-five hundred millions of dollars; but the dollar was of so uncertain value that no one can tell the equivalent in any sound currency. Besides this, there was the destruction of railroads, the burning of houses, the wasting of lands, and, above all, the emancipation of four millions of slaves, who had been purchased by their owners for three or four hundred millions sterling. It has been estimated that the entire cost of the war, on both sides, was not less than eighteen hundred millions of pounds sterling.

Great wars ordinarily cost much and produce little. What results had the American people to show for their huge expenditure of blood and treasure?

They had freed themselves from the curse of slavery. That unhappy system made them a byword among Christian nations. It hindered the progress of the fairest section of the country. It implanted among the people hatreds which kept them continually on the verge of civil war. Slavery was now extinct.

For three-quarters of a century the belief possessed Southern minds that they owed allegiance to their State rather than to the Union. Each State was sovereign. Having to-day united itself with certain sister sovereignties, it was free to-morrow to withdraw and enter into new combinations. America was in this view no nation, but a mere incoherent concourse of independent powers. This question had been raised when the Constitution was framed, and it had been debated ever since. It was settled now. The blood shed in a hundred battles, from Manassas to Petersburg, expressed the esteem in which the Northern people held their national life. The doctrine of States' Rights was conclusively refuted by the surrender of Lee's army, and the right of America to be deemed a nation was established for ever.

It was often said during the war that republican institutions were upon their trial. It was possible for the war to have resulted so that government by the people would ever after have been deemed a failure. It has not been so. The Americans have proved conspicuously the capacity of a free people to guide their own destinies in war as well as in peace. They have shown that the dependence of the many upon the few is as unnecessary as it is humiliating. They have rung the knell of personal government, and given the world encouragement to hope that not the Anglo-Saxon race alone, but all other races of men will yet be found worthy to govern themselves.

Terrible as the cost of the war has been, have not its gains been greater? The men who gave their lives so willingly have not died in vain. America and the world will reap advantage, through many generations, by the blood so freely shed in the great war against the Southern slave-owners.

XI.

AFTER THE WAR.

In all civil strifes, until now, the woe which waits upon the vanquished has been mercilessly inflicted. After resistance has ceased, the grim scaffold is set up, and brave men who have escaped the sword stoop to the fatal axe. It was assumed by many that the Americans would avenge themselves according to the ancient usage. Here, again, it was the privilege of America to present a noble example to other nations. Nearly every Northern man had lost relative or friend. But there was no cry for vengeance. There was no feeling of bitterness. Excepting in battle, no drop of blood was shed by the Northern people. The Great Republic had been not merely strong, resolute, enduring —it was also singularly and nobly humane.

Jefferson Davis fled southward on that memorable Sunday when the sexton of St. Paul's Church handed to him General Lee's message. He had need to be diligent, for a party of American cavalry were quickly upon his track. They followed him through gaunt pine wildernesses, across rivers and dreary swamps, past the huts of wondering settlers, until at length they came upon him near a little town in Georgia. They quietly surrounded his party.

May 10, 1865 A.D.

Davis assumed the garments of his wife. The soldiers saw at first nothing more formidable than an elderly and not very well-dressed female. But the unfeminine boots which he wore led to closer inspection, and quickly the fallen President stood disclosed to his deriding enemies.

There was at first suspicion that Davis encouraged the assassination of the President. Could that have been proved, he would have died, as reason was, by the hand of the hangman. But it became evident, on due examination being made, that he was not guilty of this crime. For a time the American people regarded Davis with just indignation, as the chief cause of all the bloodshed which had taken place. Gradually their anger relaxed into a kind of grim, contemptuous playfulness. He was to be put upon his trial for treason. Frequently a time was named when the trial would begin. But the time never came. Ultimately Davis was set at liberty.

What were the Americans to do with the million of armed men now in their employment? It was believed in Europe that these men would never return to peaceful labour. Government could not venture to turn them loose upon the country. Military employment must be found for them, and would probably be found in foreign wars.

While yet public writers in Europe occupied themselves with these dark anticipations, the American Government, all unaware of difficulty, ordered its armies to march on Washington. During two days the bronzed veterans who had followed Grant and Sherman in so many bloody fights passed through the city. Vast multitudes from all parts of the Union looked on with a proud but chastened joy. And then, just as quickly as the men could be paid the sums which were due to them, they gave back the arms they had used so bravely, and returned to their homes. It was only six weeks since Richmond fell, and already the work of disbanding was well advanced. The men who had fought this war were, for the most part, citizens who had freely taken up arms to defend the

May 23, 24,
1865
A.D.

national life. They did not love war, and when their work was done they thankfully resumed their ordinary employments. Very speedily the American army numbered only 40,000 men. Europe, when she grows a little wiser, will follow the American example. The wasteful folly of maintaining huge standing armies in time of peace is not destined to disgrace us for ever.

What was the position of the rebel States when the war closed? Were they provinces conquered by the Union armies, to be dealt with as the conquerors might deem necessary; or were they, in spite of all they had done, still members of the Union, as of old? The rebels themselves had no doubt on the subject. They had tried their utmost to leave the Union. It was impossible to conceal that. But they had not been permitted to leave it. They had never left it. As they were not out of the Union, it was obvious they were in it. And so they claimed to resume their old rights, and re-occupy their places in Congress, as if no rebellion had occurred.

Mr. Lincoln's successor was Andrew Johnson, a man whose rough vigour had raised him from the lowly position of tailor to the highest office in the country. He was imperfectly educated, of defective judgment, blindly and violently obstinate. He supported the rebels in their extravagant pretensions. He clung to the strictly logical view that there could be no such thing as secession; that the rebel States had never been out of the Union; that now there was nothing required but that the rebels, having accepted their defeat, should resume their old positions, as if "the late unpleasantness" had not occurred.

The American people were too wise to give heed to the logic of the President and the baffled slave-owners. They had preserved the life of their nation through sacrifices which filled their homes with sorrow and privation. They would not be tricked out of the advantages which they had bought with so great a price. The slave-owners had imposed upon them a great national peril, which it cost them infinite toil to avert. They would take what securities it was possible to obtain that no such invasion of the national tranquillity should occur again.

It was out of the position so wrongfully assigned to the negro race that this huge disorder had arisen. The North, looking at this with eyes which long and sad experience had enlightened, resolved that the negro should never again divide the sisterhood of States. No root of bitterness should be left in the soil. Citizenship was no longer to be dependent upon colour. The long dishonour offered to the Fathers of Independence was to be cancelled. Henceforth American law would present no contradiction to the doctrine that "all men are born equal." All men now, born or naturalized in America, were to be citizens of the Union and of the State in which they resided. No State might henceforth pass any law which should abridge the privileges of any class of American citizens.

An Amendment of the Constitution was proposed by Congress to give effect to these principles. It was agreed to by the States—not without reluctance on the part of some. The Revolution—so vast and so benign—was now complete. The negro, who so lately had no rights at all which a white man was bound to respect, was now in full possession of every right which the white man himself enjoyed. The successor of Jefferson Davis in the Senate of the United States was a negro!

March 30, 1870 A.D.

The task of the North was now to "bind up the nation's wounds"—the task to which Mr. Lincoln looked forward so joyfully, and which he would have performed so well. Not a moment was lost in entering upon it. No feeling of resentment survived in the Northern mind. The South was utterly exhausted and helpless—without food, without clothing, without resources of any description. The land alone remained.

Government provided food—without which provision there would have been in many parts of the country a great mortality from utter want. The proud Southerners, tamed by hunger, were fain to come as suppliants for their daily bread to the Government they had so long striven to overthrow.

With little delay the rebels received the pardon of the Government, and applied themselves to the work of restoring their broken fortunes. Happily for them the means lay close at hand. Cotton bore still an extravagantly high price. The negroes remained, although no longer as slaves. They had now to be dealt with as free labourers, whose services could not be obtained otherwise than by the inducement of adequate wages. In a revolution so vast, difficulties were inevitable. But, upon the whole, the black men played their part well. It had been said they would not consent to labour when they were free to choose. That prediction was not fulfilled. When kindly treated and justly paid, they showed themselves anxious to work. Very soon it began to dawn upon the planters that slavery had been a mistake. They found themselves growing rich with a rapidity unknown before. Under the old and wasteful system, the growing crop of cotton was generally sold to the Northern merchant and paid for to the planter before it was gathered. Now it had become possible to carry on the business of the plantation without being in debt at all. Five years from the close of the war, it is perhaps not too much to say that the men of the South would undergo the miseries of another war rather than permit the re-imposition of that system which they, erringly, endured so much to preserve.

At first the proud Southerners were slow to accept the terms offered them. They had frankly accepted emancipation. They had learned to look upon their slaves as free men. But it was hard to look upon them as their equals in political privilege.

It was hard to see negroes sitting in the State legislatures, regulating with supreme authority the concerns of those who so lately owned them. Some of the States were unable to acquiesce in a change so hateful, and continued for five years under military rule. But the Northern will was inflexible. The last rebellious State accepted the condition which the North imposed, and the restoration of the Union was at length complete.

1870 A.D.

XII.

HOW THE AMERICANS CARED FOR THEIR SOLDIERS.

Wars have been, in general, made by Kings to serve the purposes of their own ambition or revenge. This war was made by the American people, and willingly fought out by their own hands. The men who fought were nearly all Americans, and mainly volunteers. They were regarded with the deepest interest by those who remained at home. Ordinarily, the number of soldiers who die of diseases caused by the hardships they endure is greater than the number of those who die of wounds. The Americans were eager to save their soldiers from the privations which waste so many brave lives. They erected two great societies, called the Sanitary Commission and the Christian Commission. Into the coffers of these societies they poured money and other contributions to the amount of four millions sterling. The Sanitary Commission sent medical officers of experience into the armies to guide them in the choice of healthy situations for camps; to see that drainage was not neglected; to watch over the food of the soldiers, and also their clothing; to direct the attention of the Government to every circumstance which threatened evil to the health of the army. Its agents followed the armies with a line of waggons containing all manner of stores. Everything the soldier could desire issued in profusion from those inexhaustible waggons. There were blankets and great-coats and every variety of underclothing. There were crutches for the lame, fans to soothe the wounded in the burning heat of summer, bandages, and sponges, and ice, and even mosquito-netting for the protection of the poor sufferers in hospital. Huge wheeled-caldrons rolled along in the rear, and ever, at the close of battle or toilsome march, dispensed welcome refreshment to the wearied soldiers.

The Christian Commission undertook to watch over the spiritual wants of the soldiers. Its president was George H. Stuart, a merchant of Philadelphia, whose name is held in enduring honour as a symbol of all that is wise and energetic in Christian beneficence. Under the auspices of this society thousands of clergymen left their congregations and went to minister to the soldiers. A copious supply of Bibles, tracts, hymn-books, and similar reading matter was furnished. The agents of the Commission preached to the soldiers, conversed with them, supplied them with books, aided them in communicating with friends at home. But they had sterner duties than these to discharge. They had to seek the wounded on the field and in the hospital; to bind up their wounds; to prepare for them such food or drink as they could use;—in every way possible to soothe the agony of the brave men who were giving their lives that the nation might be saved. Hundreds of ladies were thus engaged tending the wounded and sick, speaking to them about their spiritual interests, cooking for them such dishes as might tempt the languid appetite. The dying soldier was tenderly cared for. The last loving message was conveyed to the friends in the far-off home. Nothing was left undone which could express to the men who gave this costly evidence of their patriotism the gratitude with which the country regarded them.

It resulted from the watchful care of the American Government and people, that the loss of life by disease was singularly small in the Northern army. There never was a war in which the health of the army was so good, and the waste of life by disease so small.

When the war was over, the Americans addressed themselves, sadly and reverently, to the work of gathering into national cemeteries the bones of those who had fallen. The search was long and toilsome. The battle-ground had been a continent, and men were buried where they died. Every battle-field was searched. Every line by which an army had advanced, or by which the wounded had been removed, was searched. Sometimes a long train of ambulances had carried the wounded to hospitals many miles away. At short intervals, during that sad journey, it was told that a man had died. The train was stopped; the dead man was lifted from beside his dying companions; a shallow grave was dug, and the body, still warm, was laid in it. A soldier cut a branch from a tree, flattened its end with his knife, and wrote upon it the dead man's name. This was all that marked his lowly resting-place. The honoured dead, scattered thus over the continent, were now piously gathered up. For many miles around Petersburg the ground was full of graves. During several years men were employed in the melancholy search among the ruins of the wide-stretching lines. In some cemeteries lie ten thousand, in others twenty thousand, of the men who died for the nation. An iron tablet records the name of the soldier and the battle in which he died. Often, alas! the record is merely that of "Unknown Soldier." Over the graves floats the flag which those who sleep below loved so well. Nothing in America is more touching than her national cemeteries. So much brave young life given freely, that the nation might be saved! So much grateful remembrance of those who gave this supreme evidence of their devotion!

XIII.

ENGLAND AND AMERICA.

America looked to England for sympathy when the rebellion began. England had often reproached her, often admonished her, in regard to the question of slavery. The war which threatened her existence was a war waged by persons who desired to perpetuate slavery, and who feared the growing Northern dislike to the institution. The North expected the countenance of England in her time of trial. It was reasonable to expect that the deep abhorrence of slavery which had long ruled in the mind of the English people would suffice to decide that people against the effort to establish a great independent slave-empire.

Most unfortunately, that expectation was not wholly fulfilled. The working-men of England perceived, as by intuition, the merits of the dispute, and gave their sympathy unhesitatingly to the North. In the cotton-spinning districts grievous suffering was endured, because the Northern ships shut in the cotton of the South and deprived the mills of their accustomed supply. It was often urged that the English Government should take measures to raise the Northern blockade. Hunger persuades men to unwise and evil courses. But hunger itself could never persuade the men of Lancashire to take any part against the North. So genuine and so deep was their conviction that the Northern cause was right.

But among the aristocratic and middle classes of England it was different. Their sympathy was in large measure given to the South. They were misled by certain newspapers, in which they erringly trusted. They were misled by their admiration of a brave people struggling against an enemy of overwhelming strength. They were misled by an unworthy jealousy of the greatness of America. Thus unhappily influenced, they gave their good wishes to the defenders of the slave-system. The North felt deeply the unlooked-for repulse. An alienation of feeling resulted which will not be completely effaced during the life-time of the present generation.

A variety of circumstances occurred which strengthened this feeling. A few weeks after the fall of Fort Sumpter, England, having in view that there had been set up in the South a new Government which was exercising the functions of a Government, whether rightfully or otherwise, officially acknowledged the undoubted fact, and recognized the South as a belligerent power. This the North highly resented; asserting that the action of the South was merely a rebellion, with which foreign countries had nothing to do. A few months later the British mail steamer *Trent* was stopped by a rash American captain, and two gentlemen, commissioners to England from the rebel Government, were made prisoners. The captives were released, but the indignity offered to the British flag awakened a strong sentiment of indignation which did not soon pass away. Yet further, there was built in a Liverpool dockyard a steam-ship which it was understood was destined to serve the Confederacy by destroying the merchant shipping of the North. The American Ambassador requested the British Government to detain the vessel. So hesitating was the action of Government, that the vessel sailed before the order for her detention was issued. For two years the *Alabama* scoured the seas, burning and sinking American ships, and inflicting enormous loss upon American commerce. These circumstances increased the bitter feeling which prevailed.

All good men, on both sides the Atlantic, earnestly desire that England and America should be fast friends. It was possible for England, by bestowing upon the North that sympathy which we now recognize to have been due, to have bound the two countries to each other inalienably. Unhappily the opportunity was missed, and a needless estrangement was caused. But this is not destined to endure. England and America now understand each other as they have never done before. The constant intercourse of their citizens is a bond of union already so strong that no folly of Government could break it. It may fairly be hoped that the irritations which arose during the war will gradually pass away, to be succeeded by a permanent concord between the two sections of the great Anglo-Saxon family.

XIV.

REUNITED AMERICA.

Long ago thoughtful men had foreseen that a permanent union between slave communities and free communities was impossible. Wise Americans knew that their country could not continue "half slave and half free." Slavery was a fountain out of which strife flowed perpetual. There was an incessant conflict of interests. There was a still more formidable conflict of feeling. The North was humiliated by the censure which she had to share with her erring sisters. The South was imbittered by the knowledge that the Christian world abhorred her most cherished institution. The Southern character became ever more fierce, domineering, unreasoning. Some vast change was known to be near. Slavery must cease in the South, or extend itself into the North. There was no resting-place for the country between that universal liberty which was established in the North, and the favourite doctrine of the South that the capitalist should own the labourer.

The South appealed to the sword, and the decision was against her. She frankly and wisely accepted it. She acknowledged that the labouring-man was now finally proved to be no article of merchandise, but a free and responsible citizen. That acknowledgment closed the era of strife between North and South. There was no longer anything to strive about. There was no longer North or South, in the old hostile sense, but a united nation, with interests and sympathies rapidly becoming identical. It has been foretold that America will yet break up into several nations. What developments may await America in future ages we do not know. But we do know that the only circumstance which threatened disruption among the sisterhood of States has been removed, and that the national existence of America rests upon foundations at least as assured as those which support any nation in the world.

The fall of slavery relieved America from the chief hindrance to her progress, and the country resumed her career of peaceful industry. The ten years which followed Mr. Lincoln's first election witnessed great changes. The population of thirty-one millions had grown to forty millions, and was increasing at the rate of a million annually. From all European countries the enterprising and the needy flocked into the Eastern States. Asia was sending her thousands to the West—the first drops of an ample shower—beneficial alike to her that gives and her that takes. Every year three hundred and fifty thousand emigrants sought a home in the Great Republic. The annual earnings of the people were estimated at two thousand millions sterling. There were forty-eight thousand miles of railroad in operation, and twenty thousand miles in course of formation. The iron highway stretched across the continent, and men travelled now in five or six days from New York to San Francisco. Notwithstanding the enormous waste of the war, the wealth of the people had nearly doubled. And yet the great mass of the rich lands which America possessed lay unused. Of nearly two thousand millions of acres only five hundred millions had been even surveyed. In the vast residue—yet useless to man—the Great Father had made inexhaustible provision for the wants of his children.

Although slavery had fallen, many evils remained to vex the American people. The debt incurred in putting down the rebellion was large, and taxation was oppressive. The paper money in which commerce was conducted was of fluctuating and uncertain value. Worst of all, there were selfish and unwise laws enacted with the view of raising the prices of articles which were largely used by the people, in order that the men who made these articles might become rich. Under these laws American trade languished and the people suffered. Everything became unnaturally dear. America could no longer build ships; she could no longer compete in foreign markets with countries whose policy was more enlightened than hers.

America has still something to learn from the riper experience and more patient thinking of England. But it has been her privilege to teach to England and the world one of the grandest of lessons. She has asserted the political rights of the masses. She has proved to us that it is safe and wise to trust the people. She has taught that the government of the people should be for the people and by the people.

Let our last word here be a thankful acknowledgment of the inestimable service which she has thus rendered to mankind.

www.ingramcontent.com/pod-product-compliance
Lightning Source LLC
Chambersburg PA
CBHW031251250426
43672CB00029BA/2097